The Malaise of Academic Scholarship

Previous books by John J. Hampton:

Culture, Intricacies, and Obessions in Academia: Why Colleges and Universities Are Struggling to Deliver the Goods

The Professoriate Today: Languishing in Dante's Purgatory

Liberal Arts in the Doldrums: Rethink, Revise, and Revitalize to Reverse the Trend

The Malaise of Academic Scholarship

Why It Starts with the Doctoral Dissertation as a Baptism of Fire

John J. Hampton

ROWMAN & LITTLEFIELD
Lanham • Boulder • New York • London

Published by Rowman & Littlefield
A wholly owned subsidiary of
The Rowman & Littlefield Publishing Group, Inc.
4501 Forbes Boulevard, Suite 200, Lanham, Maryland 20706
https://rowman.com

Unit A, Whitacre Mews, 26-34 Stannary Street, London SE11 4AB, United Kingdom

Copyright © 2018 by John J. Hampton

All rights reserved. No part of this book may be reproduced in any form or by any electronic or mechanical means, including information storage and retrieval systems, without written permission from the publisher, except by a reviewer who may quote passages in a review.

British Library Cataloguing in Publication Information Available

Library of Congress Cataloging-in-Publication Data

Includes an index.
ISBN 978-1-4758-4025-4 (cloth : alk. paper)
ISBN 978-1-4758-4026-1 (pbk. : alk. paper)
ISBN 978-1-4758-4027-8 (electronic)

∞ ™ The paper used in this publication meets the minimum requirements of American National Standard for Information Sciences Permanence of Paper for Printed Library Materials, ANSI/NISO Z39.48-1992.

To Dr. Richard Ognibene Sr., formerly of Seton Hall University and Siena College and always a scholar, who provided considerable, important input in developing the reforms recommended in this book

Contents

Preface	ix
Acknowledgments	xv

I: The Big Picture of Scholarly Research

1. Who Is Affected by the Misdirection of Academic Scholarship? How Are Harvard, Fordham, Southern New Hampshire, and the University of Phoenix Doing? — 3
2. What Are Contingent Faculty? Do They Have Anything to Do with Scholarly Research? — 9
3. What Is Scholarly Research Anyway? Professors Do It but What Are They Doing? — 17
4. When Does Scholarly Research Achieve Its Highest Satisfaction? Do I Really Want to Keep on Doing This Stuff? — 27
5. Is Scholarly Research an Affliction Weakening the Academy? Perhaps an As-Yet Unclassified Disease? — 37
6. Why Are Dissertations the Tipping Point for Scholarly Research? Is This Really Where It All Starts? — 49

II: Reforming the Doctoral Dissertation

7. Do You Have the Smarts to Do Scholarly Research? Are Weaklings Allowed in This Club? — 63
8. Why Is a Dissertation the Starting Point of Academic Scholarship? Do You Need to Know About Validity, Reliability, and that Other Stuff? — 73

9 Why Are We Fussing about Data, Information, and Knowledge? Is It Worth Our Time and Trouble?   81
10 Where Can You Find Hints and Tips for Writing a Dissertation? Don't You Want to Do It Right the First Time?   89
11 Do Scholarly Researchers Have Their Own Language? Where Is a Translator When We Need One?   101
12 Does a Quantitative or Qualitative Dissertation Make More Sense? Do You Want to Know the Answer Now or After You Attempt It?   109
13 How Does Sampling Produce Valid Findings? Does Anybody Believe What We Learned?   117
14 Why Are Limitations as Important as Findings? Do We Need to Explain that which We Didn't Learn?   123

III: Candidates Only: Practical Tips for Writing Dissertations

15 Why Is a Dissertation like Flying a Fighter Jet? Is It Enough to Take Off or Do You Want to Be Sure You Can Land?   129
16 What Is the Dilemma of the Dissertation Topic? Why Is It So Important to Resolve It?   137
17 How Can an Advisor Help Create a Workable Proposal? Do We Have Any Tips or Tricks to Share with the Candidates?   145
18 We Know Corruption Is Bad but Is It a Suitable Topic for a Doctoral Dissertation? How Should We Decide?   153
19 Have You Heard Any Good Dissertation Stories Lately? Would You Like One to Finish This Journey?   161
20 How Should You Structure a Dissertation? Is It Important to Know Where You Are Going?   167

Index   171

About the Author   177

Preface

We have a serious problem, captured in an incisive quote by Woody Allen:

> More than any other time in history, higher education faces a crossroads. One path leads to despair and utter hopelessness. The other, to total extinction. Let us pray we have the wisdom to choose correctly.

Alright, maybe a little dishonesty is going on.

The quote is not about the academic scholarship. It led off a fictional "Speech to the Graduates" written by Woody Allen for the *New York Times* in 1979. It refers to mankind and was made in a comedy context. Still, it reminds us that we need to choose the right path when we come to any juncture in the road. We are at that point in dealing with the future of academic research in today's colleges and universities.

HIGHER EDUCATION TODAY

College is not what it used to be. The academy is no longer isolated from the rest of society. Some students attend full time with professors in small classes. Most do not.

Today's colleges serve many purposes. Society is unrealistic in its expectations of what they can do. Finances come into play. Most students need help. How will they cover tuition? Are they borrowing too much? Time pressures compound the anxiety.

ASPECTS OF THE CRISIS

We are in the midst of serious troubles in our colleges and universities. To understand them, we must distinguish elite, less elite but respected, public, private nonprofit, and private for-profit schools. Our discussions can encompass difficulty or ease of admission, excessive tuition, unstable or inadequate funding, low graduation rates, poor preparation of students, and hiring part-timers or graduate assistants to teach classes. All of these issues have been extensively vetted.

SCHOLARLY RESEARCH

One area, largely ignored, deals with academic scholarship, scholarly research, and scientific inquiry. It involves the research undertaken by doctoral candidates and professors. The characteristics include:

- Goal: Careful study of a subject to discover facts or principles.
- Format: Writing using a specific formal format according to a style guide.
- Assumptions: Everything in the universe is linked by cause and reaction. There is a logical explanation for all observed behavior.

A researcher starts by making an initial assumption. A hypothesis asserts the existence of a meaningful relationship between two phenomena. A null hypothesis claims no relationship. Then the researcher seeks to prove or disprove assertion using a formal methodology. If high-powered mathematical or data manipulation tools are employed, the research is quantitative. Otherwise, it's considered to be qualitative.

Question:
   It sounds good so far. What's the relationship between scholarly research and the difficulties in higher education?
Answer:
   Simply, the activity of scholars and the standards for measuring their work have been hijacked. Colleges and universities are rewarding the wrong behaviors as they ignore their central purpose.

The evidence is compelling.

SOKAL HOAX

One professor decided to expose the situation. Alan Sokal is a professor of mathematics and physics with appointments at University College London and New York University. Widely published in the most prestigious journals, he became something of a legend when he wrote a paper titled "Transgressing the Boundaries: Towards a Transformative Hermeneutics of Quantum Gravity." After publication in 1996 by Duke University Press, Sokal told the world the paper was "left-wing cant, fawning references, grandiose quotations, and outright nonsense."

Question:
What was Sokal's purpose in publishing the paper?
Answer:
His stated goal was to attract attention to a decline of standards of rigor in scholarly research. Can a professor publish anything after developing a reputation as an academic scholar?

Apparently so.

Question:
What's the lesson learned from Sokal's paper?
Answer:
Arguably very little. His hypothesis? Scholarly research could get published in 1996 even if it is nonsense. We already knew that. It's still true today. That's one of the factors at the heart of today's problems in higher education.

Question:
Do we have evidence that Sokal's message is still relevant today?
Answer:
Yes, as recently as May 2017, when Cogent Social Sciences published an article titled "The Conceptual Penis as a Social Construct." The paper argues that the conceptual penis is better understood "as a social construct isomorphic to performative toxic masculinity." One extended quote cites fictitious articles by nonexistent authors.

> This tendency to use socially-unacceptable language is easily explained by extrapolation upon McElwaine (1999), who demonstrates clearly that, "Sexual identity is fundamentally used in the service of hierarchy; however, according to Werther (1977), it is not so much sexual identity that is fundamentally used in the service of hierarchy, but rather the dialectic, and hence the defining characteristic, of sexual identity. The subject is contextualised into a subcultural desituationism that includes sexuality as a reality."

HOW DID IT START?

The problem with academic scholarship begins upon entry into a doctoral program. It is full blown in the monumental effort of the dissertation. For most candidates, scholarly research is a battlefield. The soldier goes to war, experiences the tragedy of conflict, and is changed forever. So be it for the doctoral candidate.

PREMISE OF THIS BOOK

The problem of scholarly research is not that it's rigorous. The issue is that the dissertation's overemphasis on obscure research undermines the subsequent scholarship expected of professors in our colleges and universities. In our discussions, we will observe distinctions.

- The scope of the examination largely covers humanities, social sciences, business, and education.
- We include doctorates only if they require a dissertation.
- We are not talking about science, technology, engineering, and mathematics (STEM).
- We include efforts that are virtually never read or referenced outside a tiny circle of researchers and do not advance academic discourse in colleges and universities.

We will tackle the task of improving academic scholarship generally, and dissertation expectations specifically, in three parts:

Part I, "The Big Picture of Scholarly Research." A description of the realities of scholarly research today.

Part II, "Reforming the Doctoral Dissertation." A discussion of reforms in doctoral programs to improve the value of and process to complete a doctoral dissertation.

Part III, "Candidates Only: Practical Tips for Writing Dissertations." A section for doctoral candidates with practical tips for writing dissertations.

ESCALATOR SPEECH (FIFTEEN SECONDS)

Most scholarly research in the arts, social sciences, business, and education does not support the mission of higher education. It does not contribute to developing values and critical thinking and often encourages hiring the wrong instructors to work with undergraduate students. The problem starts with the process of creating a doctoral dissertation, and this is where the academy needs to look to make reforms.

ELEVATOR SPEECH (THIRTY SECONDS)

The often mundane and excessive requirements for scholarly research in the arts, social sciences, business, and education are undermining the professoriate and weakening efforts to provide students with a sound general education. Starting with their dissertations, professors are encouraged to produce obscure research at the expense of personal learning interactions with students. The result undermines undergraduate education. This book proposes reforms to the dissertation process.

HIGH-RISE ELEVATOR SPEECH (SIXTY SECONDS)

"When you are in a hole, stop digging." The wisdom of Will Rogers, American humorist, seems to be forgotten with respect to scholarly research in the arts, social sciences, business, and education. Why do doctoral candidates and professors produce scholarship that minimally advances knowledge and has no impact on producing educated and productive citizens? Rarely seen outside a closed club of scholars and journals, scholarly research serves only to demonstrate mastery of an art form that is not relevant in the mainstream of higher education. This book proposes reforms starting with the doctoral dissertation.

Acknowledgments

A small circle of scholars made the major contributions to this book by pointing out the fallacies of so much of current research while recognizing the real value of scholarship that improves the lessons we present to our students. The contributors include professors, doctoral candidates, and deans who take the time to improve what they do by doing it right. A thank you also goes to Tom Koerner and his colleagues at Rowman & Littlefield, who saw the value in a treatise that seeks only to improve what we do in the academy.

I

The Big Picture of Scholarly Research

Chapter One

Who Is Affected by the Misdirection of Academic Scholarship? How Are Harvard, Fordham, Southern New Hampshire, and the University of Phoenix Doing?

> It was the best of times, it was the worst of times, it was the age of wisdom, it was the age of foolishness . . . it was the season of Light, it was the season of Darkness, it was the spring of hope, it was the winter of despair.
> —Charles Dickens, English author

ELITE COLLEGES

A Tale of Two Cities arguably contains the greatest opening lines of any book in history. Written by Charles Dickens in 1859, it applies to higher education today. If your child obtains admission to Harvard or other schools near its exalted status, it's a blessing for parents whether they are drinking cocktails with the wealthy in Palm Beach or Malibu, struggling to pay bills in middle America, or overcoming obstacles so their children obtain a quality education in an urban school district.

Most students don't go to elite colleges. Seventy-one percent of 2016 high school students enrolled in a college after graduation. The Ivy League got much of the attention but accounted for only 1 percent of those graduates (see table 1.1).

Table 1.1. U.S. High School Graduates (2016)

	Total Graduates	Enrollees in College	Percent
All Schools	3,100,000	2,200,000	71%

Ivy League Admissions (Class of 2020)

	Applications	Admissions	Percent
Cornell	45,000	6,000	13%
Harvard	39,000	2,000	5%
UPenn	39,000	3,600	9%
Columbia	36,000	2,200	6%
Brown	32,000	3,000	9%
Yale	31,000	2,000	6%
Princeton	29,000	1,900	7%
Dartmouth	21,000	2,100	10%
Total	272,000	22,800	8%

Percent of Total in the Ivy League

	Enrolled	Ivy League	Percent
	2,200,000	22,800	1%

Source: http://www.businessinsider.com/2016-ivy-league-schools-ranked-by-selectivity-2016-3

If the Ivy League is great cocktail party banter, the societal impact is minimal. The Ivy League works hard to make sure every accepted student has the financial resources to attend. Still, using Harvard as a benchmark, the 5 percent of applicants who are accepted come largely from affluent homes (table 1.2).

For well-endowed and elite colleges and children and parents from financially solvent homes, it's the best of times. For almost everyone else, the times are not so good. We can look at the situation from the perspectives of individual institutions.

Table 1.2. Family Income of Harvard Undergraduates

	Below $30,000	Above $100,000	Above $200,000
Family Income			
Percent of Students	4%	82%	46%

Source: http://www.thecrimson.com/article/2017/1/25/harvard-income-percentile/

Fordham University

In 2017, the faculty members at Fordham University voted no confidence in Joseph McShane, the university's president and a Jesuit priest, by a margin of 431 to 57. The vote was a response to a reduction in faculty salary and benefits. After the vote, the president sent a message to parents and students:

> Fordham. We are an ambitious university . . . a place where talent is nurtured, character is formed, hope is born, and leaders are prepared for service to others.

At the same time, Father McShane emailed members of the Fordham community:

> The vote in no way diminishes the high regard that I have for the faculty or the pride I have in all that they have achieved in their research.

Question:
Did Father McShane see a link between the research done by the faculty and the nurturing of talent and formation of character?
Answer:
It does not matter. Each message resonates with its target audience. Parents and students react positively to "character is formed . . . hope is born . . . leaders are prepared." Faculty members are somewhat comforted by "high regard . . . their research." For them the missing ingredient is "give you more money."

Question:
Do the messages fit the context of Fordham as a university with a strong focus on faculty research?
Answer:
A good question. The message for parents and students depends on a belief that the faculty prepares leaders. Does their research help in this effort? One way to judge is to examine the five dissertations approved by the Fordham faculty in the months prior to the vote. The titles are:

- "Black Racial Identity Protecting against Stereotype Threat on Collegiate Academic Achievement"
- "Missing Covariates in Causal Inference Matching: Statistical Imputation Using Machine Learning and Evolutionary Search Algorithms"
- "Exploring Strategy Use for Multiplication Problem Solving in College Students"
- "Personal Investment, Academic Motivation, and Achievement among Early Adolescents in Trinidad and Tobago"

- "Principals' Perceptions about District Involvement in a School Improvement Initiative"

To some people, the scholarly research of the faculty has little to do with forming character, encouraging the birth of hope, or preparing students for leadership roles.

The Fordham View of Scholarship

Fordham University values scholarly research. Full-time instructional employees make up more than 50 percent of the faculty. Ninety percent have tenure or are eligible for tenure after seven years. These individuals have reduced teaching loads if they publish. Ten percent of full-timers are non-tenure-track instructors. The school employs 850 part-timers.

Southern New Hampshire University (SNHU)

Like everyone else, SNHU seeks messages that resonate:

- "Online degrees that get you where you want to go."
- "You have goals. Southern New Hampshire University can help you get there."
- "We believe there are no limits on what you can do."

SNHU also realizes that slogans are not enough. *Fast Company* magazine identified SNHU as "one of the world's 50 Most Innovative Companies."

Dramatic change began when Paul LeBlanc took the presidency of SNHU in 2003. He and the faculty recognized disruption from technology and social trends that were changing the landscape of higher education. They worked together to change undergraduate education:

- Admissions. Potential students no longer completed applications and waited for decisions. The old system: An online application would sit on someone's desk for a week. The new system: The university responds immediately.
- Customer Relations. Once accepted, students are assigned to advisers who stay with them throughout their entire program.
- Technology. SNHU added software to track students facing difficulties and monitor positive and negative teacher and student interaction.
- Facilities. SNHU created a separate and well-staffed operations center to respond quickly and effectively to commuter and distance learning students.

- Attitude. LeBlanc and staff members are not resting on current success. LeBlanc explained, "We want to create the business model that blows up our current business model . . . if we don't, someone else will."

Question:
How did it work for SNHU?
Answer:
Pretty well, if growth is any measure. By 2017, 61,000 students were enrolled in 100 graduate, undergraduate, and specialty skill programs. This compared to 3,000 students registered on campus.

The SNHU View of Scholarship

SNHU does not embrace traditional academic scholarship as it pursues its mission. Of its 4,500 instructional faculty, only 3 percent are full-time employees with faculty status. Scholarly researchers need not flaunt their writings if they apply for a position.

The University of Phoenix (UOP)

This for-profit institution has an open enrollment policy requiring only a high school diploma for admission. It offers associate, bachelor's, master's, and doctoral degrees. Its ninety or so campuses enroll 140,000 students, served by an academic staff of 16,000 personnel. A large portion of tuition is financed by student loans. One estimate is current and former students owe $35 billion to the federal government.

Question:
Is the UOP struggling in the current crisis in higher education?
Answer:
Could be. From a peak of 600,000 students in 2010, the school enrollment is precipitously down. More than 100 campuses closed as the government accused the school of taking advantage of military veterans. More than 90 percent of the classes are taught by part-timers. Only 16 percent of undergraduates receive a bachelor's degree in six years compared to the national average of more than 50 percent.

The UOP View of Scholarship

It's safe to say that the UOP is not a promising place to pursue scholarly research. Although it had 1,000 or so full-time and 20,000 or so part-time instructional faculty at its peak, research was not a front burner activity for most of them.

Question:

Do potential professors recognize the difference among Harvard, Fordham, SNHU, and the UOP when they apply for a position?

Answer:

Maybe yes, maybe no. Do they realize that Harvard chooses only "superstars," Fordham chooses largely persons interested in scholarly research, and SNHU and the UOP choose part-timers?

CONCLUSION

Different things are happening with respect to scholarly research at these schools. Fordham emphasizes scholarship even as it tries to reconcile relatively insignificant research with its mission to develop leaders. SNHU and UOP are teaching "factories." SNHU appears to be more successful than UOP. Harvard is Harvard.

Chapter Two

What Are Contingent Faculty? Do They Have Anything to Do with Scholarly Research?

> Personally, I am in favor of education but a university is not the place for it.
> —Tom Stoppard, British playwright and screenwriter

Question:

It's 11 p.m. in Manhattan and theaters near Times Square are letting out. Many residents of the city don't own cars or at least won't pay $30 a day to park them nearby. Are taxis available?

Answer:

Who cares? Click on your smartphone to request a convenient, inexpensive, and safe service to take you home. Immediately coming to mind is the ubiquitous Uber, but it's not your only choice. Lyft gives Uber a run for its money. Even taxicab companies finally adopted the model.

Higher education may be the taxicab companies of ten years ago. The business of colleges and universities is being disrupted, but the threat is masked by abuses by for-profit colleges. Their misbehavior is widely known, and it has poisoned the well.

ABUSES STARTED THE CRISIS

Colleges were slow to respond when Joshua Woods, a doctoral student at Michigan State University, dramatically exposed misbehavior in 2006. He fictitiously applied to six MBA programs as part of a research project. He used bad grammar and spelling while explaining he was a thirty-one-year-old high school graduate with a grade point average of 2.0.

Michigan State promptly answered. "An applicant must have a bachelor's degree to apply for an MBA program. More information is available on our website." Not the answer from for-profits.

Within thirty days, he was being recruited by ITT Technical Institute, the University of Phoenix, Davenport University, the American Graduate School of Management, and Corinthian College. Thirty separate emails contained four sales themes:

- Opportunity. "The starting salary for individuals holding the MBA degree is $55,000."
- Ease. "We give you all the help you need to get an MBA, including federal loan financing."
- Encouragement. "You can do it. You can improve your life."
- Shame. "Are you happy with your life? Embarrassed to tell others where you work?"

Many students responded to such admonishments. To make things worse, students were often loaded up with loans to pay tuition, the financial ramifications of which cast a shadow over higher education. By 2016, 44 million borrowers owed $1.4 trillion in student loan debt. The average was $37,000 per student.

The size of student loan debt exceeds the ability of many students and parents to repay. Delinquency rose from 6 percent historically to 15 percent by 2014. The bulk of the borrowing was by students in for-profit or lesser-known schools. The college degree was not enough to get good-paying jobs. By 2014 only 25 percent of graduates ages twenty-two to twenty-six were employed in jobs they prepared for while in college. Others were even less fortunate. More than half of those who started college quit before receiving a degree.

The overhang of debt on today's generation of Millennials will have repercussions for the next fifty years.

DISRUPTION IN THE ACADEMY

Adding to the crisis is the "taxicab"-style disruption to how the academy delivers its benefits. Are colleges responding to new realities? Did Purdue University send out a wakeup call in 2017 when it acquired the for-profit Kaplan University with its 32,000 online- and campus-based students on fourteen campuses in seven states? The *Washington Post* reported that the purchase was an effort to "extend Purdue's reach into online and adult education."

The effort by Purdue raises an interesting possibility. Colleges that disrupt the traditional model—use technology, create attractive new programs, respond to economic and other forces—may be the survivors in a world in which higher education must overcome financial and other difficulties attacking the traditional education model.

Who Will Be Affected?

We already pointed out the immunity of elite institutions to the changing business model. It's a different story for others.

- Tuition-Dependent Private Colleges. They struggle to cover the cost of providing an education at affordable levels of tuition.
- Public Universities. They try to handle all of the students who seek their lower tuition programs as legislatures cut their budgets
- Community Colleges. They thrive in terms of the number of students even as they battle for funds from state governments or local tax appropriations.
- For-Profit Colleges. After past abuses, they are targets for reform or closure.

In 2015, the U.S. Department of Education identified 500 colleges experiencing financial problems. In 2017, some observers predicted the likely closing or merging by 2023 of as many as 400 of the nation's 2,100 four-year, nonprofit colleges and universities.

FACULTY CRISIS

The financial strain on institutions and their students has created a crisis in the ranks of the faculty. There are two categories:

- Continuing Faculty. Individuals who have renewable, tenure-track, or tenured appointments.
- Contingent Faculty. Part- and full-time with little or no commitment to retain the individual as a long-term employee.

The term "contingent" implies something that happens by chance or is accidental or fortuitous. The term makes it sound like the appointment of a contingent professor is random, unpredictable, unforeseeable, or even haphazard. None of these things are even on the table. Colleges and universities strategically employ contingent faculty. The status hides under titles such as adjunct, lecturer, faculty associate, or even graduate assistant and part-time instructor. All of them, part-timers included, may teach the equivalent of a full-time course load.

Question:
So what does "contingent" mean if it is not descriptive?
Answer:
Contingent is a euphemism that hides the distinguishing characteristic of the category.

ISSUES WITH CONTINGENT FACULTY

The institution is appointing a faculty member while making little or no long-term commitment to the individuals so hired. Contingent faculty have no assurance of continuation after a short period of time, cannot receive tenure, and are not eligible for many traditional faculty benefits. They are often paid at a fraction of the level of the full-time faculty.

The availability of so many people willing to be contingent faculty creates serious problems for doctoral-prepared individuals who seek careers in the academy. Financially struggling schools have economic incentives to hire them.

Question:
Many observers argue that colleges hire contingent faculty as a conscious economic decision. Is this true?
Answer:
Perhaps, but others including the prestigious American Association of University Professors (AAUP) point out that it may not be totally a matter of economic necessity. Even schools that have lots of money hire a large number of contingent faculty. In the United States, they teach more half of all college courses including those at schools with hundreds of millions of dollars of endowment funding.

The AAUP objects to the "excessive" use of contingent faculty. The organization does not address another driving motivation to switch from research-oriented professors to classroom teachers. Is it all about money?

Question:
Is it true that contingent faculty are typically paid only for the hours they spend in the classroom?
Answer:
Yes, but the same is true for continuing faculty who have a research priority. Untenured faculty particularly must pay attention to publishing. Teaching can become a distraction.

Question:
Contingent faculty are often hired on the spur of the moment with little evaluation. Does this matter?
Answer:
This may be offset by a reality that they are hired primarily to teach, not conduct research. Many observers believe that adjunct faculty members do a better job in the classroom than tenured or tenure-track professors.

Question:
Does the high turnover among contingent faculty members mean that some students may never have the same teacher twice?
Answer:
This has positive and negative outcomes. Students can be hurt if multiple required courses are taught only by a single professor.

Question:
Does the use of contingent faculty mean that students may not be able to find instructors who know them well enough to write letters of recommendation?
Answer:
This may or may not be true because many part-timers teach lower-level general curriculum courses while recommendations tend to be written by professors in upper-level major courses.

Question:
Does overuse of contingent faculty hurt the integrity of teaching as tasks are divided and assigned piecemeal to instructors, lecturers, graduate students, specialists, researchers, and administrators?
Answer:
This is a curious concern with no easy way to verify it. The accusations of harm also include the advising of students, setting curriculum, and service on college-wide committees.

STAKEHOLDER VIEWS ON CONTINGENT FACULTY

Everybody knows the AAUP opposes contingent faculty. What's the view of others? Let's make a guess.

- Department Chair and Dean. Probably agree with the AAUP but for different reasons. It's a pain in the neck to hire six to eight adjuncts to cover

the courses assigned to a single professor. Let's hire one person, assign him or her to the same basic courses every year, and be done with it.
- Academic and Other Vice Presidents. They don't necessarily care, except maybe the finance vice president, who is trying to save a buck, and any other vice presidents who hope hiring part-timers will free up more funds for athletics, computers, or something else.
- The President or Trustees. They do not care. That's not what they do or why they took their positions.
- Students. They may prefer part-timers who are interested in teaching rather than tenured or tenure-track professors who care mostly about research.
- Parents and Politicians. They think it's horrible that part-timers teach their children and constituents. They do not know the issues and are not really that interested in them. They just want a school with a good reputation. The other stuff doesn't matter if nobody brings it up.

TENURED AND TENURE-TRACK FACULTY VIEWS

We can only imagine the views of the professors themselves. This obviously is a mixed bag.

- Tenured Professor, Superstar. Does not care. Too busy to bother with peripheral issues, students, or colleagues who are being trampled in the dust.
- Tenured Professor, Struggling to Stay Relevant. Not his or her issue. A lot of other things to do.
- Tenured Professor, Inactive Researcher. May be interested in teaching. May not. Definitely not interested in the problems of contingent faculty.
- Tenured Associate Professor Seeking Promotion. Worried about campus politics. Does not need to offend tenured professors or the dean. Not interested.
- Tenured Lifetime Associate Professor. Has given up the fight or has nothing left to do but fight. Could go either way.
- Tenure-Track Assistant Professor. Keep your head down, write and submit articles to journals, and get tenure and promotion. Not your issue.
- Contingent Faculty. A living nightmare for those seeking a career in the academy. Got to get out of the trap. Anxiety and stress. Thank God for selective serotonin reuptake inhibitors (SSRIs) such as Lexapro, Luvox, Paxil, Prozac, and Zoloft.

The reduction of tenure-track and tenured professors and explosive expansion of contingent faculty are shots across the bow of higher education. The academy demands from full-time permanent faculty teaching, scholarship, and service. It only demands teaching from nonpermanent faculty.

Question:
How do tenured and tenure-track faculty view the importance of teaching, scholarship, and service?
Answer:
Whatever the view, the rhetoric is that scholarship is the most, and in many cases the only, important factor in promotion to full professor.

Question:
What's the institutional view of teaching, scholarship, and service?
Answer:
As articulated by presidents, deans, and the faculty handbook, they are balanced. As evidenced by the demand for scholarly research as a requirement for permanent status, not so balanced. As demonstrated by a dramatic percentage increase employing contingent faculty, only teaching is of much value to many institutions.

Question:
So what's the lesson learned because colleges and universities are replacing traditional faculty with contingent faculty?
Answer:
The foundation is laid for a discussion of the role of the faculty in the current business model and the changing reality with respect to scholarly research in the future.

A DISRUPTIVE VIEW ON ACADEMIC SCHOLARSHIP

From all these premises and vantage points, we can consider another view of contingent faculty. For many it's almost the unthinkable. Phrased succinctly,

> Is it possible that much of the use of contingent faculty arises from institutions spending excessive amounts of money to support obscure and often-useless scholarly research?

We will approach this topic carefully using current evidence and a recommendation for reform of the process of writing a dissertation.

CONCLUSION

It's difficult to avoid evidence that the value system for academic scholarship is under siege in higher education. Contingent faculty are a growth industry creating serious problems to the balance of teaching, scholarship, and service. Many values deeply held in higher education are lost if institutions weaken the mentoring link between professor and student. At the same time, continuing support for the current model of scholarly research needs to be seriously examined. We continue this path.

Chapter Three

What Is Scholarly Research Anyway? Professors Do It but What Are They Doing?

> If you steal from one author it's plagiarism; if you steal from many, it's research.
> —Wilson Mizner, American playwright and raconteur

Question:
Scholarly activity is a personal choice. Some people want to do it. Some are willing to do it. Some can't do it. Some may even hate the thought of doing it. Where do we find these individuals?
Answer:
All can be found among the current students and faculty of college and universities.

Question:
Are leaders born or made? Many scholars address this question and continue to argue about the answer. Do they ask the same question about themselves? Are scholars born or made?
Answer:
It's a pretty safe bet that no one is born who intuitively knows how to do scholarly research. A bright and creative child may have thoughts about the world but his or her thinking and writing may never meet high scholarly standards.

Chapter 3
ACADEMIC SCHOLARSHIP

In the academy, scholarship consists of formal principles and practices that produce valid and trustworthy knowledge to advance a field of study. It involves rigorous inquiry, is creative and documented, and can be replicated or elaborated upon by other scholars.

The process of scholarly research is largely learned over a length of time, sometimes quite painfully involving years of effort. Once attained, the ability can be passed on to the next generation of scholars. Key terms include:

- Inquiry. Any process that has the aim of augmenting knowledge, resolving doubt, or solving a problem.
- Scholarly Research. The pursuit of knowledge following a formal process.

Academic scholarship builds upon reasoning dating from the work of Aristotle:

- Approximation. Useful knowledge is obtained from imprecise premises.
- Exactitude. Useful knowledge is obtained from precise, usually mathematical, premises.

Researchers desperately need to distinguish the two types of reasoning. When we deal with numbers, we can expect more precision than when we deal with theories or language.

Question:
   Einstein was a young man when he presented his theory of relativity. Can scholarly research prove this description of Einstein is a true statement?
Answer:
   Only if we use approximate reasoning whereby the term "young" includes thirty-seven years of age.

Academic scholarship follows one of three approaches:

- Deductive. From a theory to an explanation.
- Inductive. From the data to the development of a theory.
- Abductive. From an observation to a statement of the most likely explanation.

Question:
   At a conference, Professor Patel presented her findings that contradict the research of Professor Martino. Without reflecting upon the evidence, a student of Martino objected strongly. Why did she do this?
Answer:

Using abductive reasoning, she felt compelled to support her mentor.

These discussions lead us to four broad descriptions of academic scholarship:

- Quantitative Research. Systematic, empirical investigation of observable phenomena via statistical, mathematical, or computational techniques.
- Qualitative Research. Understanding underlying reasons, opinions, and motivations.
- Deductive Research. From the theory to the support for the theory.
- Inductive Research. From the data to develop the theory.

Question:
A research study surveys three hundred college admissions officers on their beliefs about the importance of high school grades in college acceptance decisions. Is this a quantitative or qualitative research effort?
Answer:
It's qualitative even though statistical tools may be used to present or enhance findings. A quantitative study on the same topic would compare standardized test scores or high school grades with positive and negative admissions decisions and draw conclusions from data, not perceptions.

Question:
A researcher wants to measure the change in the skills of new lending officers. He designs two parallel tests to measure the ability to diagnose signs of likely fraud by applicants for credit cards. The first test is administered upon initial hiring and the second after one year on the job. This test meets the standards for which of the following among repeatability, reproducibility, causal analysis, and inductive research.
Answer:
Maybe all of them with severe limitations. For causal analysis, the experiment does not control for additional information gained away from the job. For inductive research, a small sample and limited data are being derived to develop a theory.

SCHOLARLY RESEARCH

Scholarly research produces a document written by an expert in a field interpreting theories, data, or information. The outcome presents findings that seek to represent a significant addition to our knowledge in a specific field of learning.

Published in scholarly journals, books, or on websites, scholarly research differs from other substantive writings that are reliable sources of information. It's decidedly different from popular articles reflecting experiences, events, tastes, or entertainment of the general public because it pursues a rigorous and exacting process to improve our understanding of how things work. It augments, extends, corrects, or refutes knowledge in conceptual areas, including:

- General Knowledge. That which can be widely known by individuals or humankind.
- Discipline Area Knowledge. From prior investigation, observation, or experience that help us understand specific research areas.
- Formal Knowledge. Evidence and findings from advanced schooling or research.
- Academic Knowledge. To advance the understanding in a specialized discipline or field of study.

AREAS OF SCHOLARSHIP

Scholarly research divides broadly into two formats:

- Descriptive. Describes a population or phenomenon. It does not necessarily answer questions about how, when, or why.
- Causal. Seeks to understand the effect of one variable on another.

To perform research, we choose a methodology:

- Quantitative. Gathers information and develops findings largely based on measurements and mathematical analysis of preexisting data or new data collected through polls, questionnaires, and surveys.
- Qualitative. Gathers information from writings, questionnaires, interviews, and observation and analyzes it seeking to understand underlying reasons, opinions, and motivations.
- Mixed Method. Uses qualitative and quantitative data and methodologies.

Question:
   A researcher interviewed all recipients of an innovation award from 2002 to the present day seeking to understand the percent that support five claims of a specific theory. Which research methodology is being used?
Answer:
   Could be mixed method if statistical analysis is applied to the responses.

GROUNDED THEORY STUDY

Grounded theory is an inductive research method that starts with a question or unformatted data and searches for repeated ideas, concepts, or elements. It codes them into patterns, concepts, or categories and forms an explanation or theory from it.

Using a highly systematic methodology, the researcher reviews collected data seeking repeated ideas and concepts. Once identified, the elements are tagged and grouped into concepts and categories. These categories may become the basis for a new theory. This approach is the reverse of deductive research seeking to confirm or refute an existing belief.

One additional approach to scholarly research recognizes two broad discipline categories:

- Business, Arts, Social Sciences, and Education (BASSE). These disciplines are a "family" of research methodologies that study human society, social relationships, economics, and politics. The emphasis tends to be stronger on qualitative rather than quantitative findings.
- Science, Technology, Engineering, and Mathematics (STEM). These branches of knowledge require considerable mathematics and/or science skills. The research tends to be more quantitative than qualitative.

Most of the discussion in this book deals with the BASSE area of scholarship. We support and seek reform in the role of BASSE research as it creates the next generation of professors.

- Shut down the Spanish Inquisitions aspects of completing a dissertation.
- The effort can be rigorous without the trivial nonsense and aggravation.
- BASSE scholarly research should continue to be formidable in its pursuit of knowledge.
- Direct it to improve the behavior and success of people and institutions.

AREAS OF BASSE RESEARCH

A variety of research approaches can be found in BASSE scholarship:

- Theoretical Research. Develops, explores, or tests theories or ideas about how the world operates.
- Empirical Research. Observes and measures reality based on written or oral perceptions of people.
- Nomothetic Research. Studies classes or cohorts of individuals to understand ideas or behaviors of a larger population.

- Idiographic Research. Examines an individual seeking to understand properties that make him/her unique.
- Descriptive Research. Identifies characteristics of a population or phenomenon.
- Experimental Research. Employs a procedure to support, refute, or validate an idea, theory, belief, or relationship.
- Correlational Research. Investigates the connection between two or more variables.
- Causal Research. Compares the effect of one variable on another.
- Probabilistic Research. Adds a measure of the likelihood of an outcome based on using probability theory within the confines of a research effort.

Question:
A research study examines the life and behaviors of Archimedes to understand why he was so mathematically advanced. What category of research does this fit?
Answer:
Idiographic and empirical seem to be the best fit.

Question:
A research study examines sociological factors that supported the shift from utilitarianism to humanism in Renaissance Italy. What is the category of research?
Answer:
Perhaps theoretical or causal.

Question:
A research study collected the views of forty-five physicians on psychological factors that promote healing after an injury. What is the category of research?
Answer:
Empirical but maybe also descriptive, correlational, or causal.

Question:
A research study examined the failure of political forecasters to predict the results of the 2016 U.S. presidential election. What is the category of research?
Answer:
Maybe causal and probabilistic.

Question:
If you have to choose, would you prefer to perform correlational or causal research?

Answer:
Many researchers argue that causation is far more difficult because of hidden variables and an expectation of a higher standard of proving a relationship.

CATEGORIES OF ACADEMIC SCHOLARSHIP

In 1990 Ernest Boyer, an American educator, identified four broad categories:

- Scholarship of Discovery. Traditional research to advance knowledge. Historically this effort had been the center of academic life and was critical to an institution's reputation.
- Scholarship of Integration. Synthesizes information across disciplines or time periods. This research uses concepts and original works to create new patterns or expand knowledge into new contexts.
- Scholarship of Application. Uses existing knowledge to verify, modify, and improve prior research. It undertakes collaboration and evaluation by peers and other parties.
- Scholarship of Learning. Improves the transfer of knowledge from teacher to student or facilitates learning. It promotes active rather than passive approaches to teaching and learning.

Colleges and universities recognize all four categories, although every school ranks and accepts them differently based on its mission and philosophy.

SCHOLARLY RESEARCHERS

The creation of scholarly research is a big job. A limited range of people are involved with it. Mostly they are doctoral candidates, professors, would-be professors, and individuals who work in government, industry, and/or nonprofit organizations. Almost no one else does it. Why would they? It's usually a great deal of work to make a minor point.

MOTIVES TO CONDUCT SCHOLARLY RESEARCH

Academic research is a mandatory activity for professors who seek advancement in the academy. A professorial career has clearly marked steps like climbing a ladder. The only issue is how high a person wants to go. We know the rungs:

- Doctoral Candidate. This is a starting point. You are admitted to a doctoral program, take courses, pass written exams, and complete a dissertation. The process takes three years on rare occasions, five to seven years on average, and ten or more years occasionally, or you quit without a degree.
- Assistant Professor. The newly minted doctor accepts a relatively low-paying position. During the next seven years, the individual pursues tenure, a semi-guaranteed lifetime appointment, and promotion to associate professor, a semi-meaningless advance in stature.
- Associate Professor with Tenure. Things get easier until you feel the need to be a "full" professor. Advancement requires more scholarly research.
- Full Professor. Bingo. You did it. Despite the still-inadequate salary and routine behavioral expectations, it's pretty good to be here.
- College Administrator. Enough for teaching and research. You are eligible to be a dean, academic vice president, or even college president. Not because you want any of these positions and even because you could a good job in them. It's more money. You will get more money. You wrote a dissertation and followed it up with material that was accepted as scholarly. That's all you need.

AUTODIDACT ROUTE TO ACADEMIC SCHOLARSHIP?

An autodidact is a self-taught person. This term commonly identifies someone who studies a single subject without the guidance of professors or institutions. Notable autodidacts include Leonardo da Vinci, Charles Darwin, Srinivasa Ramanujan, and Thomas Edison. In more recent times, nominees are Jimi Hendrix, David Bowie, Steven Spielberg, and Quentin Tarantino.

In 2008, the *ABA Journal* published "Abe Lincoln's Self-Study Route to Law Practice—A Vanishing Option." The article explained that it was still possible in a few U.S. states to pass the bar and work as an attorney without ever attending law school. In 2006, 44 percent of self-study candidates passed.

An autodidact can be a lawyer. If you pass the bar, you are admitted to the practice. You can be an assistant professor of business law and receive tenure. Your writing can be considered academic scholarship if published in law journals.

Question:
Do many professors achieve their status based on being autodidacts?
Answer:
Not according to easily available information. Wikipedia produces a list of autodidacts that contains 140 names. The word professor is used only three times:

- Harlan Ellison, an award-winning fiction author and screenwriter. Not a professor himself. Wikipedia reports he punched an Ohio State professor who criticized his writing. He was expelled as a result of the incident.
- Robert Lewis Shayon, a radio producer, author, and television critic. For twenty years, he taught graduate courses at the University of Pennsylvania. He lacked a college degree.
- Benjamin West, American astronomer, mathematician, and professor at Rhode Island College, now Brown University. He only had a few months of training by a minister but was a professor from 1788 to 1799.

Question:
Do many professors achieve high scholarly research status based on possessing only a master's degree or doctoral-level preparation without completing a dissertation?
Answer:
No is a pretty safe answer, even as we do not have scholarly research to confirm it.

Question:
How important is it to complete a doctoral degree program with a required dissertation if you want to have your scholarly research accepted in the academy?
Answer:
Really important. Let's go out on a limb with it. A professor who lacks a doctoral degree with a required dissertation is an autodidact in the academy.

Question:
Does anyone ever succeed in obtaining the doctoral degree only to quit academic scholarship?
Answer:
Many do, often after burning out while completing their dissertation. Others reject the politics, low pay, or stresses of the academy. They join a for-profit or nonprofit organization as an employee and conduct scholarly research to support the employer's goals. These individuals are not the subject of this book.

CONCLUSION

Academic scholarship is a world unto itself. Scholarly research produces written support or challenge to existing knowledge. It divides somewhat into math and nonmath areas. It can be categorized in terms of what it discovers, integrates, applies, or how it affects learning. It is performed by professors and researchers who usually need schools or sponsors to pay for the effort.

Chapter Four

When Does Scholarly Research Achieve Its Highest Satisfaction? Do I Really Want to Keep on Doing This Stuff?

You'd be amazed how much research you can get done when you have no life whatsoever.
—Ernest Cline, novelist

MEDIEVAL RESEARCH STRUCTURE

When it comes to scholarly research, we return to the fifteenth century and the medieval guild:

- Master Craftsman. The full professor, an experienced and confirmed expert in a field of endeavor.
- Journeyman. An associate professor learning the skills to become a master craftsman.
- Apprentice. An assistant professor, lecturer, or contingent faculty member learning basic skills while being evaluated for guild membership. The probationary period ranges from seven years to get tenure and promotion to a lifetime of fruitless toiling.
- Intern. A doctoral candidate working on a dissertation. This augmentation to the medieval guild covers the individual who works without pay to gain the confidence of a master craftsman.

28   Chapter 4

An apprentice who showed promise would advance to journeyman. He would produce a masterpiece and present it to the masters. If it was not accepted, he would be tossed out of the guild. Alternatively, he might remain a journeyman, possibly for the rest of his life.

UNHAPPY ASSOCIATE PROFESSORS

Is it worse to continue as a journeyman or seek employment in another guild? Robin Wilson, a staff writer for the *Chronicle of Higher Education*, can help answer this question. Robin wrote about the status of associate professors in an article titled "Why Are Associate Professors So Unhappy?" in 2012, describing a female professor at the College of Wooster. Seven years after earning tenure, she was working a "nonstop, crazy schedule on 6,000 different things" for up to eighty hours a week. She chaired her department, advised students, and tried "to squeeze in time for research" that will ultimately qualify her for promotion to full professor.

Question:
   Did the professor succeed in her goal for promotion?
Answer:
   We don't know. In 2012, the professor's quote was, "When I asked a few years back who could help me with my five-year professional plan, the looks I got back were: What planet are you from?" We don't know if she will make it. In June 2017, she was listed on the Wooster website as an associate professor.

Question:
   The *Chronicle* article cites national data that show that associate professors are "significantly less satisfied with their work than either assistant or full professors." The supporting data included only tenured and tenure-track faculty. A professor explains the dissatisfaction by saying associate professors realize "there has to be something more than writing research grants, publishing, and teaching." Is he right?
Answer:
   Only partly. Sure, they hate heavy teaching loads and excessive service at many colleges. For many associate professors, it's anger accompanying the daunting and dimming prospect for completing tedious scholarly research that is the overriding requirement for promotion to full professor.

Question:

A doctoral candidate completed the dissertation, accepted an assistant professor position, wrote three articles, and received tenure and promotion to associate professor. What happens next?
Answer:
The *Chronicle* article reports that many faculty members experience "the gap between expectations and the cold reality of the job." Many associate professors started out as the highest-performing students all the way through school. They earned places in prestigious graduate programs and joined the elite ranks of the professoriate. They overcame the odds in a competitive academic job market and have lifetime employment. Then reality sets in.

Question:
What reality is that?
Answer:
It's an awakening that their obscure scholarship is a dead end. This happens even to full professors who suddenly discover they hold journeyman jobs. The *Chronicle* article quotes a professor who says "a lot of people who get doctorates are idealistic. They want to change the world or study something where they think they can make a true difference." For many, it does not happen.

STAGES OF SCHOLARLY RESEARCH

Scholarship changes at the different levels in the academic guild.

- All But Dissertation (ABD). In this stage, an excessive amount of time is spent identifying unread treatises and summarizing them in a literature review. Then information is gathered and interpreted following a strict regimen. Approval at each step requires a senior faculty member to review the material. This can be a painstaking process at best.
- Assistant Professor. In this probationary period, the researcher tries to advance the dissertation effort while watching out for alligators in the swamp. Do not alienate individuals who vote on your tenure application. Try to squeeze out time to write and submit articles to journals that are unknown to you but acceptable to those who vote. Beware of pitfalls from budgetary considerations, disagreements in faculty meetings, or politics in the faculty lounge.
- Associate Professor with Tenure. In this journeyman role, teach, teach, teach, serve, serve, serve. It can go on for thirty or more years. Every day the same. Every student the same problems. Every meeting the same boredom.

- Full Professor. The good news is you did it. That is also the bad news. You now reached the top but realize you are still in the journeyman role. See "associate professor with tenure" for the details.

TENURE AND DEPRESSION

"I've got tenure. How depressing." In 2017, an associate professor wrote an article for the *Chronicle* about her midcareer malaise when she "looked behind the curtain" and saw "a whole bunch of stuff we didn't sign on for." What could she do? "The academic labor market is so tight." Scholarly research is the same tedious task everywhere. The dream to write about the subject area you love seems to be disappearing.

Question:
  So many people who dream of being full-time tenured faculty members can't find a position. What can they do?
Answer:
  Maybe they need to acknowledge that scholarly research divides into two periods, apprenticeship and liberation. Let's take a look.

APPRENTICESHIP PERIOD OF SCHOLARSHIP

Forget about the medieval guild levels of intern, apprentice, and probation. Everything up to the point of achieving tenure or other continuing appointment is a period of apprenticeship. Observe the rules or suffer.

Question:
  A faculty member applied for promotion to full professor. Her doctoral degree was in sociology but most of her publications are linked to topics in criminal justice. She had sufficient publications to meet the scholarship expectation. Did she get the promotion?
Answer:
  No. The promotion and tenure (P&T) committee considered her scholarship to be outside her field and denied promotion. Does a doctorate in sociology provide a foundation for research in criminal justice? Who cares? It makes no difference if the P&T committee rejects it.

Question:
  A political science professor sought promotion. He submitted extensive publications on the economics of budgeting to change the environment of deteriorated inner cities. Was the scholarship accepted by the P&T committee?

Answer:

No. The economics of rehabilitating factories, starting up neighborhood businesses, and encouraging small business financing was judged not suitable for a political science professor.

Question:

A P&T committee was comparing four associate professors. Only one of them could be recommended for promotion. Which one will it be?

#1. Four scholarly journal articles and a professional book.
#2. Three scholarly journal articles and three scholarly presentations.
#3. Two books and one scholarly presentation.
#4. Six scholarly presentations.

Answer:

Nobody knows in advance. Every P&T committee will have different views.

Our conclusion? It's not about you and your research goals or dreams during "apprenticeship." Follow the rules.

LIBERATION PERIOD OF SCHOLARSHIP

Whatever the doctoral candidate's experience with a dissertation and the assistant professor's struggles to achieve promotion and tenure, a new game begins when he or she achieves tenure or other continuing appointment. The choice now broadens to four kinds of legitimate scholarly research already mentioned:

- Scholarship of Discovery. Advances the frontier of knowledge in a discipline.
- Scholarship of Integration. Synthesizes information.
- Scholarship of Application. Applies concepts or theories.
- Scholarship of Teaching and Learning. Improves faculty and student interactions.

During the probationary period, faculty members must pay distinct attention to the views (expectations? psychoses?) of P&T committees. They tend to accept:

- Scholarly Journals. Original research accepted after anonymous review by other scholars.
- Conference Proceedings. Papers presented at scholarly or professional gatherings of scholars.

After the probationary period, a multiplicity of writing opportunities opens up.

- Professional Books. Related to the discipline of teaching and research.
- Professional Trade Journals. Research on concepts and trends published by associations or professional membership groups.
- General Interest Publications. Viewpoints to inform and entertain individuals that may not have expertise in the field.
- Professional Working Papers. Scholarly documents suitable even though rejected by journals.
- Book Reviews and Other Writings. Comments and interpretation of the work of others, opinion pieces, case studies, and similar documents in the discipline.

Question:
Why would you want to write for these "nonscholarly" platforms?
Answer:
For one thing, they have a wider audience. For another, be honest. Readers of scholarly journals and attendees at conferences are not really interested in your work. Rather, they seek to publish their own. For the most part, no one is reading your stuff just as no one read your dissertation.

Question:
If you don't write for scholarly journals and conferences, will you get promoted to full professor?
Answer:
Maybe not. Probably not? This is a consideration.

Question:
How are you "liberated" without promotion to full professor?
Answer:
Some people aren't. The rank of full professor at a middle-range school matters to no one except the struggling associate professors. Many instructors, assistant professors, and associate professors who have continuing appointment have escaped the trap of obscure research. They are doing things they love, whether teaching, serving, or writing, and ignore the nonsense of rigid politics and elite posturing.

Question:
So where do we find the liberation period of scholarship?
Answer:

It's all in your head. Other than a few dollars more a month, if you are doing the things you love with your students, writing, and colleagues on campus, why does it matter?

VIEW OF DOCTORAL SCHOLARSHIP

The following shares a view of how to approach a doctoral dissertation and then pursue scholarship for tenure and promotion.

DISSERTATION PHASE SCHOLARSHIP

The four categories of "liberated" scholarship—discovery, integration, application, and teaching—do all apply to dissertation candidates equally well. The dissertation primary research emerges from secondary concepts in the literature review. The candidate might consider viewing the choices to maximize the likelihood of succeeding with the research effort.

- Scholarship of Discovery. For most candidates, this is difficult to the point of being horrific. If you have a new theory in mind, get the degree before trying to change prior research.
- Scholarship of Integration. You are well prepared after reviewing past research to synthesize it. Pick a narrow slice. Add to the field. Graduate.
- Scholarship of Application. You are also prepared to take prior research and test it. Once again, narrow, significant if not incredible, and you finish.
- Scholarship of Teaching. In the words of a native New Yorker, "fuhgeddaboudit," except for doctoral programs in education where it's a practical choice.

POSTDOCTORAL SCHOLARSHIP

After getting the doctoral degree, researchers can continue scholarship of integration and application but can consider:

- Scholarship of Discovery. Now you have a lifetime to write the masterpiece desperately needed in your academic discipline.
- Scholarship of Teaching and Learning. Even professors outside the school of education can make meaningful contributions to our understanding of how people learn.

PUBLISHING YOUR DISSERTATION FINDINGS

Every successful doctoral candidate wants to publish the final dissertation. All that work and nobody reads it? That's not good.

Question:
   How much effort should be expended to publish a dissertation?
Answer:
   Not much. Do not attempt to publish your dissertation!

This is an unacceptable and even insulting suggestion for a newly minted doctoral graduate. Doesn't everyone want to know in some detail what you found out in seven years of study? After all, your dissertation is titled "The Influence of Otto Weininger on the Moral Understanding and Phenomenology Reflected in the Writings of Ludwig Wittgenstein." Who would not be interested in that?

The reality is nobody cares about either Otto or Ludwig. A better idea is to use the foundation of knowledge from your dissertation to create articles. Start with the most significant finding. Describe it and do a little more work with it. Use your literature review as a foundation for a suggestion on further research. Seek a reputable journal and try to get an article published.

DISSERTATION QUICK START

We have detailed help in future pages. For the moment, you are encouraged to write a dissertation following a careful step-by-step process that does not wander. For BASSE dissertations, one approach is:

- Prior Knowledge. What do I know already? What is the area of my discipline that interests me the most?
- Pick a Topic. In that area, what puzzles me, arouses my curiosity, or represents a problem that needs to be solved?
- Vet the topic. Do I see a gap in current knowledge, an update that is needed, or an otherwise worthwhile issue to examine? Would it be interesting to investigate it? Would the results be significant?
- Hypotheses. What are four to six questions I would answer?
- Primary Research. How would I answer them?
- Significance. Why is my finding to each question significant? Who would care?

Write up in less than three pages the answers to these questions. Then work with the school to find an advisor who agrees with you on the effort. In consultation with the advisor, submit the proposal or start the research.

CONCLUSION

Scholarly research achieves its highest satisfaction when a scholar studies and writes about topics and in styles that meet personal needs to understand and create knowledge. In many, if not most, cases, it's separate from the rigid definitions in the academy. The professor begins to realize the most satisfaction occurs at schools where scholarship is valued in a proper balance with teaching and service.

Chapter Five

Is Scholarly Research an Affliction Weakening the Academy? Perhaps an As-Yet Unclassified Disease?

> His pretense to profound and obscure scholarship, his blundering ventures in stilted and labored pseudo-humor, and his often-vitriolic outbursts of critical prejudice must all be recognized and forgiven.
> —H. P. Lovecraft, author and editor

Lovecraft's quote, a criticism of the writing of Edgar Allen Poe, could easily be applied to much of today's scholarship. Minus the part about pseudo-humor. Scholarly research is devoid of humor of any kind, but that is not its only characteristic. Let's look.

THE HIDDEN AILMENT

As already noted, colleges and universities are dealing with a variety of challenges and issues. Less attention is given to an illness in the body of the academy. Simply expressed, scholarly research is a malady attacking the heart of colleges and universities. The "medical" evidence is everywhere. We need to confront the situation and treat it.

BACKGROUND TO THE CRISIS

All modern scholarship traces back to Plato's Academy in the fourth century BC. It flourished with new ideas about art, literature, justice, politics, education, family, friendship, and love. It created the foundation for Western philosophy, science, politics, religion, and economics.

Plato's academy morphed over the centuries into a Judeo-Christian framework largely identified with Europe and North America. It went through phases:

- Pre-Christian Concepts. The efforts of Socrates (b. 470 BC), Plato (b. 428 BC), and Aristotle (b. 384 BC).
- Early Christian Theologians. These include Paul of Tarsus (b. 5 BC), Augustine of Hippo (b. 354 AD), and Thomas Aquinas (b. 1225 AD).
- Renaissance Philosophers. Many great thinkers included Rene Descartes (b. 1596 AD), John Locke (b. 1632 AD), Isaac Newton (b. 1642 AD), and Immanuel Kant (b. 1724 AD).

MEDIEVAL UNIVERSITIES

Established in Italy, England, France, Spain, and Portugal, medieval universities began in the eleventh century. Professors today would be quite comfortable in thirteenth-century Oxford, Paris, or Bologna. Led by a "master," a student took four years for a bachelor's degree and six years for a master's. Studies were organized by a faculty and covered philosophy, mathematics, physics, astronomy, grammar, logic, and music. Much of the instruction was given in Latin.

The topics were clustered under what came to be known as the liberal arts. Today the spectrum contains four fields:

- Arts. Includes art, literature, philosophy, religion, ethics, languages, music, theater, and speech.
- Social Sciences. Such as history, geography, psychology, sociology, political science, and economics.
- Natural Sciences. Examples are biology, chemistry, physics, and earth science.
- Formal Sciences. A grouping that includes logic, mathematics, statistics, and computer science.

PROFESSORS AS THE HEIRS OF PLATO

To make sense of the academy, we must recognize that professors follow in the footsteps of Plato. Platonic education helps society achieve:

- Individual Justice. Excellence when every student seeks to develop his or her ability to the fullest.
- Social Justice. Harmonious relationships among workers, warriors, and rulers.

The academy promotes Platonic education and thus is arguably the most important institution in a just society.

The professor is the key to the academy. The title identifies one who has a special knowledge of a philosophy, art, behavior, or skill and shares it with young people. The professor leads the search for justice, so students will try to do their best and, as citizens, pursue harmony with others.

Question:
When did it go wrong?
Answer:
When scholarship replaced learning as the most important component of being a professor.

DEVELOPMENT OF TODAY'S SCHOLARSHIP

The professoriate is the top tier of the academy. Reaching it can be problematic even for an educated adult. Once upon a time, professors and nurses shared a common destiny. There was a shortage of both. Sure, the pay was low given the mandatory expectation of a higher education degree and a display of basic competency. Achieve these entry-level credentials and all were welcome. You could play by the rules and be confident of lifetime employment. Or at least having a job until you burn out, retire, or die.

RAISING THE PROFESSORIATE BAR

Sometime in the 1980s, the rules changed. Not so much for nurses, where a shortage of practitioners kept up demand. Nursing was not attractive. Doctors and hospitals expected nurses to work hard during an extended career. No such problem for professors. After getting tenure, life could slow down.

The professoriate had its own challenges. Many aspirants saw the career as an opportunity to write and reflect. Yes, some teaching was required, but unlike teaching in a high school or community college, it was tolerable.

As the profession attracted more and more people, we saw an interesting reaction to the surplus of individuals who sought to populate it. Following a strategy employed by labor unions, hiring, promotion, and tenure committees raised the standards for admission to and retention in full-time tenure-track positions.

The two critical measuring tools were teaching and scholarship. Professors did not seem to have much concern about the teaching component. Scholarship became the focus. The academy overemphasized scholarly research and used it as a tool to block entry and permanent status.

ADMINISTRATOR AGREEMENT WITH "HIGHER" STANDARDS

The emphasis on scholarship resulted in a harmony of faculty and administration, two groups that, like the mongoose and the snake, often seem to be mortal enemies.

- Faculty. Professors had control of their ranks. The new standards did not apply to them. Although members P&T committees often had limited scholarly achievement, their positions took on an aura of elitism.
- Administrators. Presidents and deans could reduce the costs of their operations. They could hire less credentialed or part-time teachers to fill classrooms and replace them after a few years with new lower-paid instructors.

The outcome, for the moment at least, is the best of times for full professors with tenure. It's the worst of times to be trying to reach that status. "Many are called, but few are chosen" (Matthew 22:14). More than half of college courses are taught by lecturers, instructors, and part-time teachers who replaced the assistant, associate, and "full" professors of thirty years ago.

SUCCEEDING AS A SCHOLAR

What does an aspiring professor do to succeed in the academy? Many books answer this question. Often their focus is not complete. You want to be a professor? Get a doctorate with a dissertation. Produce scholarly research if you are lucky enough to get a tenure-track position. Everything else is a diversion, a distraction, or as has been suggested by U.S. political rhetoric, an "alternative truth."

An axiom of higher education for many years has been the requirement of a professor to produce and disseminate scholarly research. Does such effort pay off? We can ask Jacques Berlinerblau, a professor at Georgetown University. Well, we don't have to. In May 2017, he gave examples of the role of academic scholarship. Mostly in his words:[1]

- "These days, it's not unusual to find a department where a bloated full professor, age 72, has been out-published by a scrawny adjunct, age 35. . . . To survive she published obscene quantities of peer-reviewed research. The graybeard, by contrast, received tenure decades ago. Back in the 70s, one could get hired and promoted for flossing regularly. The older scholar makes about five times as much as the adjunct. Naturally, he teaches half as many classes."

- "Amanda and Irene were best friends in grad school. . . . They worked under the same doctoral adviser. They possess nearly identical publication records. . . . Yet Amanda teaches part time at a community college and . . . Irene has a tenure-track job at a top research university. Their relationship has grown strained."
- "Professor Welch . . . has been laboring for a quarter-century on a seminal study. . . . Colleagues . . . recount tales of his epic labors, his devotion to craft, his personal sacrifices. . . . Welch has not yet published his masterpiece. . . . In fact, he hasn't published anything . . . since the fall of the Iron Curtain that coincided with his being granted tenure."
- "Deadwood blossoms among Ivy. World-class sprinters labor at schools considered also-rans. Welch is revered in his field. Much more so than Boris . . . who churns out four workmanlike, peer-reviewed articles per decade. Welch sits on well-regarded editorial boards. Boris sits in his tiny, windowless office double-checking his footnotes. . . . Welch is consulted by nonprofits that dole out grant money to humanists. But not humanists like Boris."
- "Professorial prestige, I contend, is an awfully arbitrary thing."

Question:
What do the words of Professor Berlinerblau say about academic scholarship?
Answer:
All's not well. It's not appreciated. Not administered with equity. Not logical.

Question:
In 1905, at the age of twenty-six, Albert Einstein developed the theory of special relativity and proposed the mass-energy equivalence in the formula $E=mc^2$. He earned his PhD in the same year with a dissertation that contained findings of much less significance than several other writings. Did he need to write the dissertation?
Answer:
Maybe not. If you are a person that others frequently compare to Einstein, maybe you could succeed at Princeton University without a doctoral degree. Otherwise, achieving one with a dissertation is highly recommended no matter how significant your scholarship.

WHO READS SCHOLARLY RESEARCH?

The work of scholars, whether in the form of dissertations, journal articles, or other formats, are rarely read. They may be widely cited by other scholars and this is taken as a sign that they are worthwhile. Generally, citations are based upon recommendations of other scholars, many of whom never read the original work. Why bother when a cursory review of the abstract or findings will do the job?

Question:
"He is so far above us! We can't be expected to understand him." This is a quote from movie star Bill Murray describing Dr. Richard Dreyfuss in the 1991 movie "What about Bob?" Does a failure to understand the message and language of professors apply to their academic research?
Answer:
Maybe. As an example, we can consider some of the Boston University 2016 titles of dissertations written by likely future professors. Which one sounds the most interesting?

- "Absolute Ambivalence: Sites of Collecting and Display Under Franceso I de'Medici"
- "Plasmonic Enhancement of Chiral Light-Matter Interactions"
- "Quantitative Investigation of the Activation Mechanism of the RET Receptor Tyrosine Kinase"
- "Reliable Gene Expression and Assembly for Synthetic Biological Devices in E. coli through Customized Promoter Insulator Elements and Automated DNA Assembly"
- "Enantioselective Multicomponent Organoboron Reactions of Ortho-Quinone Methide Intermediates, Catalyzed by Chiral Biphenols"
- "First Principles and Effective Theory Approaches to Dynamics of Complex Networks"
- "Point Process Modeling and Estimation: Advances in the Analysis of Dynamic Neural Spiking Data"

SCHOLARLY JOURNALS

Though rarely read, professors have many choices for where to submit. Obscure, peer-reviewed publication of research has become quite a business. We can start with Wikipedia's sixty-three separate listings of journals by topical area. Ulrich's list verifies the publication is peer-reviewed or has equivalent editorial control of quality. SENSE publishing identifies categories with rankings.

PREDATORY JOURNALS

Separately from respected journals, a predatory journal in open access publishing has been described as "an exploitative open-access publishing business ... charging publication fees to authors without providing the editorial and publishing services associated with legitimate journals." Other characteristics include:

- Notifying academics of fees only after papers are accepted.
- Aggressively campaigning for academics to submit articles or serve on editorial boards.
- Listing academics as members of editorial boards without their permission.
- Appointing fake academics to editorial boards.
- Mimicking the name or website style of more established journals.
- Misleading claims about the publishing operation.

Question:
Where can we find a list of predatory journals?
Answer:
We can't. Until 2017 the source was "Beall's List," a website report regularly updated by Jeffrey Beall, a librarian at the University of Colorado. In 2016, the list identified 1,155 open-access journals with predatory practices.

Question:
What happened to Beall's List?
Answer:
It was removed from the Internet in 2017. A colleague said professor Beall "was forced to shut down the blog due to threats and politics."

Question:
John Bohannon, a journalist, submitted a hoax article to a number of academic journals in 2013. He reported that 60 percent of them accepted the article for publication. What was the response?
Answer:
In addition to praise, the effort was criticized on scholarly research grounds. Specifically, it was not itself peer-reviewed, had a flawed methodology, and failed to employ a control group.

Question:
In 2015, Professor Anna Szust applied to 360 academic journals to be a member of their editorial boards. Her qualifications were weak with no prior

publications of her own and no editorial experience. She cited fake books, book chapters, and publishers. Did any of the journals add her to their boards?

Answer:

Yes. One-third of the "predatory" journals accepted her almost immediately. This finding was published in 2017 in *Nature* magazine as the "Dr. Fraud" experiment.[2] Researchers created a fictitious Professor Szust, giving her the Polish word for "fraud" as her name. Most of the 120 journals identified as reputable did not respond to the application. None offered her a position on the board.

Question:

Derek Pyne, an associate professor, studied the publications of faculty at his own Thompson Rivers University. Did he find articles in predatory publications?

Answer:

Using two ranking systems by outside authorities, Pyne's evaluation of thirty-eight professors revealed that predatory journal articles were previously published by:

- Every full professor, two-thirds of associate professors, and 10 percent of assistant professors.
- Seventy-five percent of full-time, tenure-track professors with research responsibilities.

Question:

Is it really necessary for professors to publish in predatory journals?

Answer:

In one way, it hardly seems necessary. With all the journals on Wikipedia, Ulrich's, and SENSE, even a mediocre researcher should have some success.

START OF THE RESEARCH AFFLICTION

The problem becomes visible if we answer a few simple questions:

- What is scholarly research? The output of an effort to publish in a specialized field of study.
- Who does it? Doctoral candidates, professors, and would-be professors or college administrators.
- Why do they do it? To climb an academic ladder.
- Who reads it? Almost no one.

Question:
You can't seriously undertake scholarly research without a doctorate. Plus, you must write a dissertation. Who says?
Answer:
Practices and behaviors in the academy. Deans and committees that make hiring decisions. Promotion and tenure committees. Editors who decide what gets published. Government agencies and foundations that award funding to support research.

Question:
Does everyone agree that autodidacts are not welcome?
Answer:
It seems like it. Colleges cite the number of doctoral faculty because parents and admissions officers seem to agree that the degree improves learning opportunities.

Question:
Do students agree on the importance of a doctorate with a dissertation?
Answer:
RateMyProfessors.com is a website where students can evaluate professors. Some students are not kind to their doctoral-qualified professors. A sample of negative comments include:

- About a political science professor: "When I actually do go to class, halfway through I begin to hate God for giving me the legs that brought me there."
- About a sociology professor: "He's a little arrogant. He went to Hahvahd. It's understandable."
- About an English professor: "Peel away the layers of his superadded bombast and you get very little, maybe a whimpering thought, a distant muffled howl, a cry for help."

Question:
Many organizations are seeking alternative routes to scholarly recognition. Universities offer free massive open online courses (MOOCs). The website selfmadescholar.com identifies free classes to help people become "amazingly informed and therefore properly opinionated." Can such efforts produce autodidacts capable of scholarly research?
Answer:
Sure, but who will pay attention to their work if they lack a PhD, EdD, or the equivalent?

Question:

What's the right place for scholarly research?
Answer:
The dissertation is the first scholarly research. Then publication in academic, refereed, or peer-reviewed journals that publish articles:

- Written by experts using specialized jargon of a discipline.
- Building on prior research by citing extensive footnotes and bibliographies.
- Confirmed for value and creative content by independent experts who recommend publication.

Question:
What are the wrong places for scholarly research?
Answer:
Publications that do not meet scholarly research standards include:

- Trade Journals. Containing practical information on developments and trends in a field of activity.
- General Interest Magazines. Providing information without vetting for accuracy.
- Popular Magazines. Publishing short, relatively easy-to-read articles with little depth to entertain, not necessarily inform, a general audience.

Question:
Are books considered scholarly publications?
Answer:
Yes, when the book is published by a university press or recognized educational publisher. Otherwise, each book must be evaluated for evidence that it's a scholarly work. Clues include:

- Respected Publisher. Does the book carry the imprint of a publishing house known for publishing serious scholarly work?
- References. Does the book cite reputable researchers, authors, articles, books, or other research reports or efforts?
- Specialized Terminology. Does the book use discipline-specific language appropriate to the field of research?
- Expert Author. Do the degrees, years of experience, and prior research mark the author as an authority in the field?

Question:
A scholar is a person who has done advanced study in a special field. Scholarship is the professional writing of such a person. Is this information sufficient for us to fully understand academic scholarship?

Answer:

Not really. If we are honest about it, scholarship in the world of academia mostly means publishing in the right places.

RIGHT PLACES TO PUBLISH?

Okay. Publish in refereed journals. Where do we find them?

- Wikipedia. Separate listings organized by topical areas. Fourteen in biochemistry, eighty-six in botany, ten in ecology, 120 in entomology, seventy-five in forestry, and so on.
- Ulrich's Peer-Reviewed List. Information about popular and academic magazines, scientific journals, and other publications. Includes editorial control of quality.
- SENSE. Publishing categories for journals and books that "provide a stimulating and supportive context for doctoral candidates and early-career researchers." Scholarship ranked as refereed, other academic, and nonacademic.

Question:

Do all the professors who want to write have outlets for their research?

Answer:

We do not know who "wants to write." We do know many professors submit articles for publication. They have lots of choices. By category, SENSE identifies 770 publishers as shown in table 5.1.

The ten top publishers are the university presses of Cambridge, Columbia, Harvard, Johns Hopkins, Massachusetts Institute of Technology, Oxford, Princeton, Stanford, University of Chicago, and Yale.

Table 5.1. Publications on SENSE List (2016)

Category	Number of Publishers
Top Publishers	10
Semi-Top Publishers	73
Other Refereed Publishers	188
For an Academic Audience	341
For a General Audience	158
All Publications	770

CONCLUSION

We defined academic scholarship in its current usage in the academy. It is nothing more than any research performed by a person holding a doctorate and seeking to meet accepted scholarship standards. It may be published as a dissertation (thesis) or as an article in a peer-reviewed or otherwise vetted journal or book that is acceptable to the academy. All other work, no matter how groundbreaking or otherwise valuable, counts. This is the affliction of scholarly research in the academy today.

NOTES

1. Jacques Berlinerblau, *Campus Confidential: How College Works, or Doesn't, for Professors, Parents, and Students* (Brooklyn, NY: Melville Publishing House, 2017).
2. Piotr Sorokowski, Emanuel Kulczycki, Agnieska Sorokowska, and Kataryna Pisanski, "Predatory Journals Recruit Fake Editor," *Nature*, March 22, 2017.

Chapter Six

Why Are Dissertations the Tipping Point for Scholarly Research? Is This Really Where It All Starts?

> The tipping point is that magic moment when an idea, trend, or social behavior crosses a threshold, tips, and spreads like wildfire.
> —Malcolm Gladwell, author

PURPOSE OF A DISSERTATION

We can discuss the dissertation . . . thesis . . . whatever you want to call it . . . in the simplest terms. What is it? What are its goals, rationale, and purpose?

Question:
   Are we talking about a dissertation or a thesis?
Answer:
   Although the terms are used interchangeably, we can make a technical distinction.

- Thesis. A hypothesis, conjecture, or theorem that advances the state of knowledge in an academic discipline. It must be an original and significant contribution.
- Dissertation. A formal, stylized document used to argue your thesis. It must be clear and complete but not exhaustively comprehensive.

The thesis makes a claim. The dissertation seeks evidence to support or refute it. The document does not "prove" anything or reveal "truth."

Question:
Why do you want to write a dissertation?
Answer:
It depends on your philosophy. Some choices include:

- Precursor to a Book. When finished it will be published as a seminal contribution to the field.
- Pet Peeve. Fix something that others simply fail to understand.
- Lifelong Dream. Complete a significant and worthwhile writing project.
- Complete Your Program. Meet the requirement so you can graduate with a doctoral degree.

Question:
Is one motivation better than the others?
Answer:
You might say so.

- Precursor to a Book. When finished, no one will read it. Even your advisor is likely to skim it. Your doctoral committee members may read only the abstract. No one will ever publish it. Well, with one exception. Send it to www.lulu.com. For less than $10 each plus shipping, you can print as many copies as you want.
- Pet Peeve. This involves emotions. The pain of writing a dissertation in a tedious format and getting it approved with campus politics in enough emotion for lifetime. Leave the baggage of pet peeves behind.
- Lifelong Dream. You will wake up from your significant and worthwhile writing project the day after is it accepted. The sun will come out or it will not.
- Complete Your Program. This is the real dream. Meet the requirement so you can graduate with a doctoral degree. Having the degree is the goal. Everything else is a distraction.

Question:
Why does the academy want you to write a dissertation?
Answer:
It is the culmination of the process of preparing a person to help others understand how the world works. Nothing more. In this context, education has five levels:

- Elementary and Middle School. Prepares citizens with foundation knowledge of the world and basic skills using words and numbers.
- High School. Enhances foundation knowledge and basic skills with a focus to prepare young people for jobs or college.

- College. Develops a higher level of critical thinking and understanding of how the world works.
- Graduate Study. Opens doors for more desirable or higher-level jobs or the opportunity to pursue or change careers where master's degrees are expected or required.
- Doctoral Study. Demonstrates through the writing of a dissertation that a person can identify a gap in knowledge, create a framework to provide evidence to address it, and write a document that supports or refutes existing knowledge.

Question:
What is the value of a doctorate if the program of study does not require a dissertation?
Answer:
It doesn't count except at cocktail parties with your friends and strangers.

Question:
Will my doctorate without a dissertation at least allow me to get a tenure-track teaching position?
Answer:
Highly unlikely at four-year institutions. At community colleges and other schools where a master's degree is acceptable for long-term appointment, the doctorate without a dissertation might marginally increase the chance of appointment.

The discussion is pretty straightforward up to this point. Create a powerful document that reflects the culmination of scholarly research skills. Graduate with the ability to advance the frontier of knowledge. Take a university or other position where you can make contributions.

The reality is different. Let's go there.

HAZING OF THE CANDIDATE

For the most part, doctoral candidates probably did not pledge a fraternity or sorority in college. They missed out on hazing—the imposition of humiliating tasks as part of a program of initiation. Neither did they go through rigorous physical torments imposed upon cadets in military academies. Late night research in the library is not the same thing.

The hazing begins at the start of the dissertation process. Professors are pleased to have one or two graduate assistants to help them with their research. They have little interest in being a "nurse maid" to a fledgling scholar. In the halls of the academy, we can almost hear the words: "I do not change diapers. Neither do I direct dissertations."

Many professors have a better attitude. "I want to help." They become overwhelmed by the task. "How many baby birds can I feed?" Soon they become discouraged by the workload and shy away from candidates.

A third group of advisors lacks the skills to be of any help. Perhaps as a result of their own dysfunctional treatment as doctoral candidates, they give the wrong advice. The candidate never gets on track, responding to a series of dead ends as the research effort unfolds.

The result is that a majority of ABD candidates never finish the dissertation. The individuals who survive the hazing take years to graduate. Data on averages from start to completion of the dissertation vary by discipline. For those who finish, the picture is not pretty. See table 6.1.

The obstacles to degree completion involve the dissertation director, health of the candidate, misunderstanding by the candidate, and the eventual onset of despair as progress slows to a crawl.

- Psychological deterioration begins when the candidate attempts to identify every shred of preexisting scholarship. The review of the literature never ends.
- It continues as the candidate submits proposals and drafts and receives conflicting and obtuse comments after lengthy and unexplained delays.
- It becomes embarrassment as family, friends, and others ask, "So how are you doing?"
- Finally, it becomes paralysis. The project stalls and then dies.

This needs to change. We need a tipping point, a powerful framework proposed by Malcolm Gladwell in his book of the same name.

Table 6.1. Time to Degree for Doctorate Recipients, CGS Communicator, March 2010

Discipline	Time to Completion
Physical Sciences	6 years
Engineering	6 years
Life Sciences	7 years
Social Sciences	8 years
Humanities	9 years
Education	11 years

TIPPING POINT IN THE ACADEMY

A tipping point is a moment in time when an unstoppable change (an epidemic) is about to occur. Characteristics include:

- Contagiousness. Circumstances create a rapidly spreading influence that excites the emotions.
- Impact. Little causes have big effects.
- Speed. Change happens in one dramatic moment.

Question:
   How do contagiousness, impact, and speed fit in to a dissertation process?
Answer:
   The doctoral committee decides to get rid of the overhang of unfinished dissertations. A few small changes can fix this by bringing together three forces:

- The Right People. Individuals who can work together to create change.
- The Right Message. Communication makes a memorable impact. Gladwell calls it a "sticky" message.
- The Right Context. A situational change that opens all the doors. Human beings are highly sensitive to the things around them. Gladwell calls this the power of context.

Question:
   Who are the right people?
Answer:
   The president, dean, and senior faculty need to work together to develop a system that helps candidates.

Question:
   Suppose the doctoral committee chair wants to change a policy that must be approved by faculty senate and academic vice president. Should he or she talk with anyone in advance?
Answer:
   According to Gladwell, he or she should talk to everyone in advance. His or her friends should make introductions, help him or her shape the reasons to support a change, and talk with others to gain support prior to the meeting where a vote will be taken.

Chapter 6
THE RIGHT MESSAGE

Gladwell reminds us that the right message must be "sticky," distinctive, and likely to motivate a positive response. We find sticky messages everywhere.

- The Best Part of Waking up Is Folgers in Your Cup (1960s)
- A Diamond Is Forever (1948)
- Wheaties, the Breakfast of Champions (1935)

Do we find them in higher education? According to George Felton, Columbus College of Art & Design, "college slogans tend to be—how to put this?—kind of lame. They sound like they were written by the admissions department or development folks on a Friday afternoon in a badly ventilated little meeting room."

With names redacted, he cites:

- University of _____. Tradition. Change. Excellence.
- Think Success. Think _____ University.
- _____ College. To Know. To Lead. To Serve. To Understand.

Slogans may not work in higher education but sticky messages are needed to tell a simple story with a sharp message. We can compare sticky with less sticky. This is how President John F. Kennedy identified the goal of making the United States the global leader in space travel:

> I believe that this nation should commit itself . . . to landing a man on the moon and returning him safely to the earth by the end of this decade.

Compare Kennedy's quote with the comparable statement from another source. Boring, boring, boring.

> The United States seeks to achieve the goal of being the international leader in the exploration of space by pursuing with determination and resolution a maximum degree of scientific knowledge, collaboration and creativity, and tactical and strategic aerospace initiatives.

Question:
  What are sticky messages for changing the dissertation process in a doctoral program?
Answer:
  How about:

- "Seventy-five percent of our ABD candidates fail to graduate."
- "Many candidates have $65,000 in debt and no degree when they quit."

- "How can someone get through all the course work and not be prepared to write a dissertation?"

THE RIGHT CONTEXT

Gladwell and others have written extensively on how big goals are often achieved by making small changes. To understand the world, we need to look at the subtle, the hidden, and the unspoken. To create a tipping point, we bring in a few of the right people, develop a compelling message, and change the context from negative to positive. Bingo. We have a tipping point.

LITTLE THINGS MAKE A BIG DIFFERENCE

In 1993, Samsung Electronics Chairman Lee Kun Hee was visiting an electronics conference in Los Angeles. He noticed that Sony stood out while Samsung was lost in the crowd. This did not please him. He returned to Korea and changed the context in the Samsung design center. A small change.

The company created a separate design center near its headquarters but not in it. It was a way to overcome the Confucian respect for elders and reluctance to speak out of turn. The unit developed its own unique culture with no dress code for workers and everyone was encouraged to speak up and challenge each other and their superiors.

The change of context worked. By 2007, Samsung was a key player in product design.

RESEARCH METHODOLOGY COURSES

Changing the context of doctoral programs starts with courses where professors explain the nature of scholarly research. The following titles and their variations can be identified in the mix.

- Understanding Research Methods
- Advanced Research Methods
- Methodologies and Data Analysis
- Mixed Methods Research
- Theory and Practice of Collective Inquiry
- Introduction to Research Inquiry
- Qualitative Methodology
- Quantitative Methodology
- Causal Analysis of Research Problems
- Analytical Methods for Research

- Experimentation and Modeling

Question:
  So what's the problem with these courses?
Answer:
  Several things.

- Doctoral programs often require four or more such courses that are not coordinated and present conflicting messages.
- Professors lack the skills to make sense out of them for a disparate group of candidates. They fail to explain quantitative methods properly to candidates working on qualitative research designs and vice versa.

Research methods courses need to be redesigned.

- Current Design—Just in Case. We encourage learning about all sorts of research methodology so everyone will know the entire field. This does not help candidates focus on how to complete their own project.
- Revised Design—Just in Time. We provide limited background and work with candidates on specific areas of interest and problem statements. If done in a classroom with multiple candidates, candidates share their stories and learn from each other as well as the professor.

Question:
  What reform is needed in the course?
Answer:
  It needs to be taken early in the program with a coach as the instructor. Candidates who do not show an aptitude for scholarship need to be identified and the school needs to deal with the problem.

Question:
  What should the school expect of the candidate?
Answer:
  The candidate should get the message. This means:

- Search for a director that you like and who likes you. Get help early.
- Complete a competent review of the literature as you work on assignments for courses. By the time coursework is finished, a candidate can have a forty- to one-hundred-page bibliography of foundation material in the area of the dissertation.
- Discuss methodology for the primary research. If more statistics courses are needed, take them.

By overlapping term papers with a likely literature review, the candidate is developing the background to write a dissertation before even finishing the coursework. This alone helps reduce the burden of the dissertation, not to mention improving a candidate's attitude in dealing with obstacles or unexpected changes.

Question:
Will it help if the advisor and candidate view the dissertation approval as something of a game?
Answer:
It might. Even under the best of circumstances, dissertation writing is akin to Whac-a-Mole. Each of the five holes on the table contains a single plastic mole that randomly pops up. Hit it on the head so it goes back into the hole and you score points. The quicker you do it, the higher your score. The prize for "academic Whac-a-Mole" is the doctorate.

Question:
Does an early start have corollary benefits?
Answer:
It does in terms of money. The cost of a doctoral program consists of components. Speed up the process and reduce borrowing and the interest on and loss of salary. The tuition alone can be formidable. Sample costs are shown in table 6.2.

Table 6.2.

Institution	Tuition and Fees
Barry	$36,000+
Capella	$56,000+
Case Western (DM Program)	$150,000+
Duke	$58,000+
Pace (DPS Program)	$70,000+
Rutgers (In-State)	$18,000+
Rutgers (Out-of-State)	$30,000+
UCLA (In-State)	$16,000+
UCLA (Out-of-State)	$32,000+
Walden	$60,000+

Source: http://www.valuecolleges.com/rankings/best-value-graduate-schools/

Question:

Does the acceptance decision by universities figure into needed reforms?
Answer:
Yeah, actually it does. The academy needs to assess awarding more than 50,000 doctorates annually.

Doctoral candidates often ignore the shortage of university jobs. Vacant full-time faculty openings are outnumbered three to one by newly minted candidates. Even more distressing is that half of all candidates fail to complete their programs in ten years. See table 6.3.

Of those who finish, only a quarter land a full-time appointment within five years of graduating. In a recent year, 100,000 people started doctoral programs, 52,000 were awarded degrees, and institutions had 15,000 vacant academic positions.

Question:
Do doctorally prepared individuals eventually find a permanent position in higher education?
Answer:
The stark fact of life is no. A late 1990s survey of individuals found many of them outside the academy ten years later. The numbers varied by discipline.

TIPPING POINT FOR THE CANDIDATE

Suppose the academy does not revise the dissertation journey. Can the candidate create his or her own tipping point? Maybe yes.

- Select a director you know and like and who likes you. Offer to help with his or her research. Do anything so the director feels motivated to help you.
- Complete a competent review of the literature and stop. Write down what you find in the prescribed format. Lock down the chapter. Do not touch it again. If someone demands that you add something, do it and lock it down again.
- Design the methodology and start doing the research. Check off the boxes in the process, normally a series of obsessive and trivial roadblocks. Dot the i's, cross the t's, and stay the course.
- Write, write, write. It does not have to be perfect. Most directors will stop reading it if you have volume.

Table 6.3. Percent in the Academy Ten Years after Doctorate Awarded (1998)

Discipline	Percent
Sciences	47%
Engineering	40%
Computer Science	57%
Humanities	73%
Mathematics	76%
Discipline	**Tenured**
Sciences	25%
Engineering	36%
Computer Science	48%
Humanities	60%
Mathematics	64%

Source: http://www.gradschoolhub.com/faqs/what-is-the-average-time-to-obtain-a-ph-d

CONCLUSION

The dissertation process needs to be reformed almost from start to finish. This involves decisions by institutions, doctoral faculty, advisors, and candidates. We need the right people, right messages, and right context to come together to achieve the goals of scholarly research while reducing obstacles and helping candidates.

II

Reforming the Doctoral Dissertation

Chapter Seven

Do You Have the Smarts to Do Scholarly Research? Are Weaklings Allowed in This Club?

> If you can't explain it simply, you don't understand it well enough.
> —Albert Einstein, theoretical physicist

Question:
　In the movie *Rain Man*, Dustin Hoffman played an autistic savant. He could calculate complex math problems as fast as a computer. He was dysfunctional dealing with basic behaviors of living. Was he a person qualified to perform scholarly research?
Answer:
　Maybe. He was mathematically a genius. Interpersonally an idiot. Some doctoral candidates claim this is the behavioral model of their dissertation advisors. Could they be right?

Question:
　The completion of a doctoral dissertation encourages the assumption that the researcher was smart. Is that true?
Answer:
　It depends on your definition of smart. If the word is synonymous with intelligent, the researcher may be smart. If your understanding is having a quick-witted intelligence, maybe not.

COGNITIVE AND EMOTIONAL INTELLIGENCE

The behavior of Rain Man illustrates two kinds of intelligence. On the one hand is a person's ability to think, reason, remember, and process knowledge. On the other is social and interpersonal behavior:

- Cognitive Intelligence. A general mental capability to reason, solve problems, and understand complex ideas.
- Emotional Intelligence. The ability to identify and manage your own emotions and the emotions of others.

Cognitive intelligence is measured by intelligence quotient (IQ), formal tests that have a median score of 100. Over 120 is superior. Two-thirds of the world's people are in the range of 85 to 115. Between 70 and 130 we find 95 percent of the world's population.

Emotional intelligence is measured by emotional quotient (EQ), also using formal tests. A typical result identifies high, medium, and low EQ.

Question:
With respect to scholarly research, what's the relationship of cognitive and emotional intelligence?
Answer:
Cognitive intelligence provides tools to grasp complex concepts. When augmented by high emotional intelligence, a researcher reduces dead ends and tortuous pathways while uncovering areas of study and producing findings.

Question:
With respect to the ability to select a viable dissertation topic, is cognitive or emotional intelligence more important?
Answer:
They may be equally important. IQ improves the likelihood of accurately identifying situations, facilitating moving from feelings and opinions to facts and beliefs, and understanding hidden messages. EQ is critical and can be decisive in managing the interaction with professors, subjects, and resource providers to produce a successful outcome.

Question:
Can a scholar increase his or her cognitive or emotional intelligence?
Answer:
Cognitive intelligence seems to be stable over time and cannot be changed. Most recent research agrees that we have the ability increase emotional intelligence.

Question:
Do people exhibit more IQ or EQ behavior in the conduct of scholarly research?
Answer:
IQ is visible everywhere; EQ often appears to be lacking.

Question:
When working with dissertation advisors, mentors, or members of a dissertation committee, is it more important to have a high IQ or a high EQ?
Answer:
Emotional intelligence has an edge:

- Perceptions. EQ can more accurately identify emotions.
- Thinking. EQ facilitates moving from feelings and opinions to facts and beliefs.
- Meaning. EQ seeks to understand hidden messages.
- Management. EQ can better manage the emotions of others.

REALISTIC VIEW OF COGNITIVE INTELLIGENCE

Scholarly research is not for the faint of heart. Nor is it likely to be successful if a person lacks the capability to deal with sophisticated concepts. Cognitive intelligence has two components: general knowledge and obscure knowledge. A scholar usually needs both.

General Knowledge

Scholarly research often arises from things seen by a scholar but not visible to others. This tendency is often shown by the breadth of a person's nontechnical knowledge. The following ten questions compiled from SAT practice questions test general knowledge of a teenager with English-language fluency in a U.S. school. How many can you confidently answer?

Are you Cognitively Smarter than an American Teenager?

1. There is no doubt that Larry is a genuine _____: he excels at telling stories that fascinate his listeners. Which of the following fills in the blank?

    a. braggart
    b. dilettante
    c. prevaricator

d. raconteur

2. A discerning publishing agent can _____ promising material from a mass of submissions, separating the good from the bad. Which of the following fills in the blank?

   a. supplant
   b. finagle
   c. winnow
   d. overhaul

3. A special lottery is to be held to select the student who will live in the only deluxe room in a dormitory. There are 100 seniors, 150 juniors, and 200 sophomores who applied. Each senior's name is placed in the lottery three times, each junior's name two times, and each sophomore's name one time. What is the probability that a senior's name will be chosen?

   a. 1 over 8
   b. 2 over 9
   c. 2 over 7
   d. 3 over 8

4. This table shows the noontime temperatures in Hilo, Hawaii, over a one-week period.

Mon	Tue	Wed	Thu	Fri	Sat	Sun
66	78	75	69	78	77	70

If "m" represents the median temperature, "f" represents the temperature that occurs most often, and "a" represents the average (arithmetic mean) of the seven temperatures, which of the following is the correct order of "m," "f," and "a?"

   a. $a < m < f$
   b. $a < f < m$
   c. $m < a < f$
   d. $m < f < a$

5. John realized that he had been _____ in his duties. If he had been more _____, the disaster may have been avoided.

   a. A. irreproachable / careful
   b. B. arbitrary / interested

c. C. neglectful / insensible
d. D. derelict / vigilant

6. When you are planning to make a left turn across an intersection and you are waiting in the middle of the intersection for the traffic to clear, your front tires should be turned

    a. to the left.
    b. it depends on the sharpness of the turn.
    c. straight ahead.
    d. to the right.

7. What is the meaning of each of these abbreviations?

    a. 2BZ4UQT
    b. ACORN
    c. ADIP
    d. BMGWL

8. The battles of Chancellorsville and Manassas were fought in what state?

    a. Virginia
    b. Pennsylvania
    c. Maryland
    d. Mississippi

9. Where would you go if you wanted to find comestibles?

    a. To a grocery store.
    b. To an atlas of the world.
    c. To nursery.
    d. To a beach.

10. A nurse must record temperatures in Celsius but her thermometer reads Fahrenheit. A patient's temperature is 100.7°F. What is the temperature in °C?

    a. 32.0°C
    b. 36.5°C
    c. 38.2°C
    d. 44.3°C

ANSWERS: SMARTER THAN A TEENAGER

1. There is no doubt that Larry is a genuine D. raconteur: he excels at telling stories that fascinate his listeners.
2. A discerning publishing agent can C. winnow promising material from a mass of submissions, separating the good from the bad.
3. There are 100 seniors, 150 juniors, and 200 sophomores who applied. Each senior's name is placed in the lottery 3 times, each junior's name 2 times, and each sophomore's name 1 time. The probability of a senior's name is D. 3 over 8.
4. The correct order is A. a < m < f.
5. John realized that he had been D. derelict in his duties. If he had been more vigilant, the disaster may have been avoided.
6. When making a left turn, your front tires should be turned C. straight ahead.
7. Meaning of each abbreviation.

2BZ4UQT	Too Busy for You Cutie
ACORN	A Completely Obsessive Really Nutty Person
ADIP	Another Day in Paradise
BMGWL	Busting My Gut with Laughter

8. The battles of Chancellorsville and Manassas were fought in A. Virginia.
9. To find comestibles go: A. To a grocery store.
10. 100.7°F equals B. 36.5°C.

Question:
How do doctoral candidates do on the test?
Answer:
Mixed except for question number seven, which hides in the world of those who text and tweet. The culture of teenager Internet communications does not seem to match doctoral candidates. Maybe they are not texting and tweeting enough.

OBSCURE KNOWLEDGE

Scholarly research is enhanced by knowing and remembering things that others forgot or never knew. The following test measures curiosity as an indicator of cognitive intelligence, once again for adults with English proficiency who graduated from American schools.

ARE YOU CURIOUS ABOUT OBSCURE FACTS?

1. Which of the following warnings did Paul Revere shout when he made his famous ride?

    a. Beware. British troops on the march.
    b. The British are coming.
    c. The Regulars are coming.
    d. People. Prepare your arms.

2. Where was American baseball first played?

    a. In Hoboken, New Jersey
    b. In Cooperstown, New York
    c. By Abner Doubleday
    d. None of the above

3. Which of the following dates marks the founding of the United States of America?

    a. July 2, 1776
    b. July 4, 1776
    c. September 3, 1783
    d. None of the above.

4. Which of the following individuals designed the American flag?

    a. George Washington
    b. Thomas Jefferson
    c. Betsy Ross
    d. Francis Hopkinson

5. Which of the following was the motive for the Puritans who came to the New World on the Mayflower in 1620?

    a. They were opposed to religious freedom.
    b. They were seeking religious freedom.
    c. They wanted to escape oppression in England.
    d. Two of the above.

6. Which of the following is the forbidden fruit eaten by Adam and Eve in a story in the Bible?

a. Pear
b. Peach
c. Apple
d. None of the above.

7. Which of the following is a binding legal opinion issued by an Islamic scholar under Islamic law?

    a. Fatwa
    b. Jihad
    c. Tazir
    d. None of the above.

8. Which of the following is not an actual word in the English language?

    a. Funnest
    b. Irregardless
    c. Thusly
    d. All of the above are recognized as English words.

9. Which of the following comes from English Common Law as the source of the expression "rule of thumb"?

    a. Banning a butcher from placing a finger on a scale to increase weight of meat.
    b. Limiting a husband's right to beat a wife with a stick.
    c. Approximating an inch as the distance from the tip to the first joint on a thumb.
    d. None of the above.

10. Which of the following was the life expectancy of a twenty-one-year-old male in medieval England?

    a. Ten more years
    b. Twenty-five more years
    c. Forty more years
    d. Fifty-five more years

ANSWERS: CURIOUS ABOUT OBSCURE FACTS

1. c. "The Regulars are coming." As most citizens considered themselves to be British, they would not react to "The British are coming."

2. d. None of the above. American baseball evolved from a variety of earlier sports.
3. c. September 3, 1783, formally ending the Revolutionary War. Maybe, A. July 2, as it was the actual date of the signing of the Declaration of Independence.
4. d. Francis Hopkinson gets most credit as she led several individuals through the process of designing the American flag.
5. a. They were opposed to religious freedom. The Puritans escaped oppression in England by going to Holland but did not like the religious freedom given to others.
6. d. None of the above. The Bible does not identify a specific fruit.
7. d. None of the above. Legal opinions issued by Islamic scholars are not binding.
8. d. All of the above are recognized in various dictionaries.
9. c. Approximating an inch by carpenters is the most likely source.
10. c. Forty more years. The average for the entire population was much lower as a result of high rates of death during childhood.

LINKAGE BETWEEN SCHOLARSHIP AND INTELLIGENCE

Who is smart enough to undertake scholarly research? Cognitive intelligence alone does not do the job in the absence of emotional intelligence. Students with "average" cognitive intelligence consistently outperform "smarter" people. A high EQ is the dominant factor explaining success in decision making, successful collaboration, and time management.

In creating new knowledge, four competencies correlate with EQ:

- Self-Awareness. A high EQ means we recognize our reactions, situations, compliments, attacks, and surprises.
- Self-Management. Our efforts to be flexible and adjust our responses in constructive directions.
- Social Awareness. The capability to accurately perceive people's thoughts and feelings even though we may not agree with them.
- Relationship Management. The skill at managing interactions with others to achieve positive outcomes.

A high EQ allows a person to achieve goals building upon a foundation of self-awareness, self-management, social awareness, and relationship management.

DISSERTATION REFORMS

The balance of EQ and IQ falls apart in many doctoral programs. Weaknesses include:

- Total Overload. A program may require roughly the equivalent of two years of course work followed by two or more years for the dissertation.
- Methodology Overload. Coursework on how to conduct research can be mind-numbing. One program requires eleven three-credit courses including Qualitative Inquiry 1 and 2, Causal Analysis 1 and 2, and Advanced Analytical Methods.
- Mentor Overload. When the candidate workload is not focused or excessive, directing an effort can overwhelm the advisor.

Sometimes the design of the program is simply overkill. One school requires candidates to synthesize a theoretical body of literature, complete a qualitative fieldwork project, and finish a rigorous quantitative empirical study prior to starting a dissertation. How much is enough? That's the question here.

CONCLUSION

Considerable evidence exists that people who complete scholarly research do better if they possess cognitive and emotional intelligence along with curiosity. When they possess these characteristics, it may be fair to also say, "They are smart." This appears to be the foundation for completing a reasonable original dissertation.

Chapter Eight

Why Is a Dissertation the Starting Point of Academic Scholarship? Do You Need to Know About Validity, Reliability, and that Other Stuff?

> The only limit to the height of your achievements is the reach of your dreams and your willingness to work hard for them.
> —Michelle Obama, American lawyer, writer, and First Lady

SHOULD YOU WRITE A DISSERTATION?

Completion of a dissertation identifies a person with the ability to propose solutions for normative problems in a specific area of academic inquiry. It advises others that you can participate in scholarly forums and activities affecting a branch of knowledge. It is the first serious effort to display scholarly research skills:

- Comprehensive Background Study. Search for prior knowledge in the area of the research.
- Significant Issue. Address a gap, need for update, or correction in prior research.
- Original Research. Conduct a formal investigation gathering data and analyzing it with modern tools and interpretation.

To conduct scholarly research, a person needs to crystalize certain concepts. Let's take a look.

LINEAR AND LATERAL THINKING

Researchers should be careful not to limit their thinking. Two focuses are needed:

- Linear Thinking. Gathers data and organizes it in a sequential structure to reach a conclusion.
- Lateral Thinking. Start with the data and augment it with intuition, imagination, risk taking, and conscious and subconscious processes.

RESEARCH REASONING

Scholars acknowledge two approaches to drawing conclusions:

- Intuition. The processing of data without identifying relationships and linkages. A person conceptualizes relationships and "feels" a course of action.
- Sequential Reasoning. The processing of data by identifying intermediate steps and linkages, organizing information and consequences, analyzing events and options, and selecting a choice.

VARIABLES

A variable is an observation or entity that can take on different values. In life, your age is a constant at any moment in time. In other situations, it's a variable as it has different values for different people or at different times.

Most scholarly research applies sequential processing tools to variables. The three categories include:

- Independent Variable. A factor or condition in a functional relationship that can change the value of another variable.
- Dependent Variable. A variable affected by another variable.
- Attribute. The specific value of a variable.

Question:
   A factory has tables where workers assemble electrical components into a finished product. A researcher is collecting data on the relationship between the level of light in the room and the speed of assembling the product. What are the independent and dependent variables?
Answer:
   The experiment was designed with light as the independent variable and speed as dependent upon it. The hypothesis was more light, more speed. This

experiment between 1924 and 1927 showed no relationship. Individuals responded to the attention they received as opposed to the degree of light. This third variable problem is called the "Hawthorne effect."

Question:
　Gender is a constant for a person but not for a population. What are the attributes of gender as a variable?
Answer:
　Male and female historically.

Question:
　Is the answer to the attributes of gender an example of linear or lateral thinking?
Answer:
　Maybe linear. If lateral thinking is applied, transgender and intersex are recent additions as attributes.

Question:
　A study can examine whether people agree on what's happening. What are the attributes of agreement as a variable?
Answer:
　One approach is 1 = strongly disagree, 2 = disagree, 3 = neutral, 4 = agree, and 5 = strongly agree.

Question:
　Is the answer to the attributes of agreement an example of linear or lateral thinking?
Answer:
　Maybe lateral would include 0 = not applicable.

ATTRIBUTES OF VARIABLES

Researchers recognize two kinds of attributes:

- Exhaustive Attributes. All possible states are included in the research.
- Mutually Exclusive Attributes. If one attribute is identified, no other attribute can be present.

Question:
　A researcher is studying the performance of college seniors with varying religious backgrounds. All students on a campus may volunteer. Before tak-

ing the exam, the students self-identify as Catholic, Protestant, Muslim, and Jewish. What is a weakness of the design of this study?
Answer:
It does not establish religion with exhaustive attributes. It should add categories such as "other" and "none."

Question:
A researcher is surveying individuals and seeks to correlate employment status with attitudes on a political issue. Before filling out the form, individuals identify themselves as employed or seeking employment. What is a weakness of this design?
Answer:
The attributes are neither exhaustive nor mutually exclusive. A person currently employed but job hunting fits both answers. A person who is unemployed and not seeking full-time employment is a distinct attribute.

RELATIONSHIPS

Scholarly research often works with the relationships among variables. Some possibilities include:

- Causal Action. It makes something else happen.
- Correlated Action. It occurs at the same time as another action.
- Positive Relationship. High values on one variable are associated with high values on the other. Low values on one are associated with low values on the other.
- Negative or Inverse Relationship. High on one is associated with low on the other and vice versa.
- No Relationship. Neither causal nor correlation.

Question:
Research shows that people with a strong capability to do math also have a high proficiency in music. What kind of relationship exists between math and musical ability?
Answer:
Perhaps a positive and correlated relationship.

Question:
A country had an annual increase of 3.5 percent in the rates of skin cancer for twenty years. Annual visitors to New York City increased by 3.6 percent over the same period. Does this indicate that visiting New York City causes skin cancer?

Answer:
No. Correlation is not causation.

Question:
A researcher determined that a positive correlation existed between the number of lawsuits filed in Europe and the number applications for law school in the United States. With a rise in European lawsuits, U.S. law schools received more applicants. Is this a positive causal relationship?
Answer:
Probably not, as lawyers certified in one country usually do not practice in another. It could arise from a third variable, such as the European lawsuits involving U.S. citizens or organizations who want U.S. lawyers to represent them.

INFERENCE IN RESEARCH

Inference refers to developing new knowledge from evidence or reasoning. The researcher uses it to move from a position considered true to another whose truth is believed to follow from it.

Question:
A researcher learned that 84 percent of respondents liked a politician in 2015. In 2016, the politician was accused of accepting a bribe. In 2017, polls showed that only 32 percent liked him. What caused the drop in popularity?
Answer:
We don't really know but we can infer that it is caused by distaste for politicians accepting bribes.

VALIDITY AND RELIABILITY

For most researchers, the dissertation is the first place where they focus on two concepts:

- Validity. The best available approximation to the reality of a proposition, inference, or assessment.
- Reliability. The degree to which an assessment tool produces stable and consistent results.

Question:
What's the relationship between validity and reliability?

Answer:
   There is none. They are independent of each other. A measurement may be valid but not reliable. It may be reliable but not valid.

The likelihood of having a valid and reliable study is enhanced by two factors:

- Reproducibility. Can it be performed again in its entirety?
- Repeatability. Does it produce similar results each time it is performed?

FORMS OF VALIDITY

If you understand the basic definition of validity, you can skip the details. In case you need to know them, here are a few terms:

- Internal Validity. Occurs when the results rule out or make alternate explanations unlikely.
- External Validity. Exists when the results can be generalized to other situations.
- Construct Validity. The research study measures what it claims to measure.
- Content Validity. The study measures all facets of what it claims to measure.
- Concurrent Validity. The measure in the study is accurate compared to the outcome.
- Predictive Validity. The measure in the study question would produce a similar outcome in a future study.

Question:
   What's the significance of the different forms of validity for scholarly research?
Answer:
   Researchers want to ensure that the study produces results that are useful. Does the research measure the right things? Are the relationships proposed by a theory correct or reasonable? Does the research cover enough area to make its findings valid? Are the findings contradicted by other research?

MEASUREMENT

Ultimately, the researcher needs to measure something in order to have significant results. The success of a researcher working with data depends on specific abilities:

- Recall. Remember prior knowledge.
- Understand. Grasp concepts.
- Apply. Use knowledge in new situations.
- Analyze. Examine methodically and in detail.
- Synthesize. Put things together.
- Evaluate. Assess the value of data.

CONCLUSION

An understanding of variables, validity, reliability, and other basic research concepts sharpens the focus of scholarly research. It is the foundation to prove cause, correlation, or other relationships in the pursuit of knowledge in a structured framework.

Chapter Nine

Why Are We Fussing about Data, Information, and Knowledge? Is It Worth Our Time and Trouble?

In God, we trust. All others must bring data.
—W. Edwards Deming, statistician

The dissertation continues a tradition of seeking the truth and this effort builds on what's known from the past. The candidate has to beware of being buried in data. The first step is to distinguish among three terms:

- Data. Raw or unorganized facts and beliefs. It can refer to words, numbers, symbols, conditions, ideas, or objects.
- Information. Data that has been refined to meet one of the following conditions:

  - It has been verified as accurate and timely.
  - It's organized.
  - It's presented in a context with meaning and relevance.
  - It can lead to an increase in understanding.

- Knowledge. A combination of valid information and researcher interpretation organized into findings for a dissertation.

Question:
   A mountain climber is preparing to ascend Mount Everest. What data, information, and knowledge might be helpful?
Answer:

82   *Chapter 9*

Data on the temperature on Mount Everest. Information on the geographical structure of the mountain. Knowledge as a set of instructions on when and how to climb the mountain.

DATA INTEGRITY

This is assurance of the accuracy and consistency of the design, collection, processing, and storage of data. Some considerations include:

- Data Corruption. Errors that occur when using data.
- Data Loss. Corruption that can occur when data is stored or processed.

DATA SOURCES

Data is generated from two broad sources:

- Primary Source Data. Created by a researcher from interviews or analysis without interpretation or evaluation by other researchers.
- Secondary Source Data. Derived from the work of other researchers.

Question:
   What's the relationship of primary and secondary source data to the literature review?
Answer:
   The literature review is totally the identification and explanation of the research of others.

Question:
   Is the goal of secondary research to identify and report on all scholarly research that underlies the dissertation?
Answer:
   Not necessarily.

- It should cover prior research that has obvious influence.
- It should create a picture of the current level of knowledge in the research area.
- It should show that the researcher has the background to conduct the primary research.

Question:
   Where is the primary source data in a dissertation?
Answer:

It's found in the research methodology and findings, not in the literature review.

DATA DISCRIMINATION

In the search for useable data, the researcher must assess its value based on its origin:

- Fact. Empirical data or an observable phenomenon supported by evidence.
- Belief. A psychological state holding a proposition or premise to be true. It's based on a combination of facts and interpretations. It may be based in the conscious or unconscious mind.
- Feeling. A complex experience when belief interacts with other factors to modify behavior.
- Opinion. A judgment created by unsubstantiated information internalized from past experience.
- Assumption. A belief that is accepted as being true without reflection or evidence.
- Bias. A perspective when a person prefers an interpretation, conclusion, or reaction.

REALITY OF DATA SOURCES

Of the six foundations for interpreting data, the researcher may start with a belief and end with the same or a different belief. Research on the data shapes beliefs. The researcher takes care to sort what's happening:

- Facts. A "fact" may or may not be true. In the collection of data, a fact provides a basis for reaching a conclusion. It should not arise from a preconceived notion.
- Feelings. By intensifying the interpretation of information, feelings distort conclusions.
- Opinions and Assumptions. Because they come from unknown or questionable experiences, they also distort conclusions.
- Bias. This prejudgment interferes with the interpretation of evidence.

Measuring with Statistics

We can use statistics to provide evidence in support of our findings. To be effective, we must count the right things and convert raw data into useful information. Malcolm Gladwell made this point in his 2005 book, *Blink: The Power of Thinking without Thinking*. His example uses two baseball players where the raw data shows either a hit or an out while batting one hundred times.

Question:
   From the raw data, can you see which player is the better hitter?
Answer:
   The batters are pretty close but Ty Cobb has a higher batting average than Tony Gwynn. It is difficult to see from raw data but easy to see when we calculate hits at 36.8 percent of the time for Cobb and 33.8 percent for Gwynn.

The lesson from the baseball example is that the researcher gets into trouble by displaying findings in tables or formulas without a clear explanation of the meaning of the data. With a dissertation, a director or committee that cannot understand the material is inclined to delay approval on a research effort.

Baseball Data Organized into Information[1]
   Raw Data:

Ty Cobb. Batting Statistics.
In 100 at-bats, the following happened:

Hit. Hit. Out. Out. Out. Out. Hit. Hit. Out. Out. Hit. Hit. Out. Hit. Out. Out. Out. Hit. Hit. Out. Out. Out. Hit. Hit. Out. Out. Out. Hit. Out. Out. Out. Hit. Hit. Out. Out. Out. Hit. Out. Out. Out. Hit. Hit. Out. Out. Out. Hit. Out. Out. Out. Out. Out. Hit. Out. Out. Out. Hit. Out. Out. Out. Hit. Hit. Out. Out. Out. Hit. Hit. Out. Out. Out. Hit. Hit. Out. Hit. Hit. Out. Out. Out. Hit. Hit. Out. Hit. Hit. Out. Out. Out. Out. Hit. Out. Out. Out. Hit. Hit. Out. Out. Out. Out. Hit. Hit. Out. Out. Out.

Tony Gwynn. Batting Statistics.
In 100 at-bats, the following happened:

Hit. Hit. Out. Out. Out. Out. Hit. Out. Out. Out. Hit. Hit. Out. Out. Out. Out. Hit. Out. Out. Out. Hit. Hit. Out. Out. Out. Out. Hit. Out. Out. Out. Hit. Out. Out. Out. Out. Hit. Out. Hit. Out. Hit. Out. Hit. Hit. Hit. Out. Out. Out. Hit. Out. Out. Out. Out. Hit. Out. Out. Out. Out. Hit. Hit. Out. Hit. Out. Out. Hit. Hit. Out. Out. Out. Hit. Hit. Out. Hit. Out. Out. Out. Out. Hit. Hit. Hit. Hit. Out. Out. Hit. Hit. Out. Out. Out. Hit. Hit. Out. Out. Out. Out. Hit. Hit. Out. Out. Out.

TELL THE STORY WITH DATA

Michael Lewis makes the same point in his *New York Times* article "No-Stats All Star" that data is not enough. It must be the right data and be properly interpreted. Does it explain relationships among variables?

Gladwell answers the question with data on Shane Battier, a professional basketball player.[2] Battier had significant achievements prior to playing professional basketball. His record is as follows:

- High School. He won the Naismith award as the best player in the United States.
- College. He repeated his high school success. His team won 131 games, the 2001 national championship, and he got another Naismith award, this time as the best college player.

Lewis and Gladwell said that statistical performance in a game is only a small part of understanding the value of an athlete. Other factors include: How hard does he work? Is he a good teammate? Is he resilient when faced with problems? How does he perform under pressure?

Shane joined the Memphis Grizzlies, a losing team in the National Basketball Association, in 2001. After one year with Shane on the Grizzlies, performance of the team improved as follows:[3]

Team Won and Loss Records

- 2001–2002: 23–59
- 2002–2003: 50–32
- 2003–2004: Made the NBA playoffs
- 2004–2005: Made the NBA playoffs
- 2005–2006: Made the NBA playoffs

Shane was traded to the Houston Rockets. Once again, team performance improved after his arrival. The won and loss record is as follows:

Before:	After:
2005–2006: 34–48	2006–2007: 52–30
	2007–2008: 55–27 (including 22 wins in a row)

Both teams got better, but did the presence of Shane Battier make a sizeable portion of the improvement? First, Gladwell examined the numbers traditionally used to measure the value of basketball players. In terms of basketball statistics, Battier's record was:

86   *Chapter 9*

- Points. Not many.
- Rebounds. Not many.
- Blocked Shots. Not many.
- Assists. Not many.
- Steals of the Ball. Not many.

INTERPRETING THE DATA

Why is Battier valuable? Gladwell explains what happens when he is on the court:

- His teammates get a lot better.
- His opponents get a lot worse.

The point is clear. Gladwell encourages researchers to measure things that are important, not things that are easy to measure. In basketball, should you take a bad shot or pass to an open teammate? Pull down a rebound or tip it to a teammate? Guard a weak player or the other team's best player?

The challenge for the researcher is to isolate the right independent variables to show causes or correlations with outcomes. The dissertation is a process of gathering and interpreting it correctly to achieve a valid and reliable outcome.

IDENTIFYING UNDERLYING FACTORS

Scholarly research can have a difficult job with underlying factors that produce the meaningful data. Examples include:

- Incomplete Data. A lack of data or not having the ability or technology to analyze it.
- Deceptive Data. Information compiled and modified to encourage a misinterpretation of what happened.
- Intensity of Data. Emotions, enthusiasm, or commitment underlying information or perceptions from data providers.

Question:
   In advance of the 2016 U.S. presidential election, pollsters predicted a 70 to 95 percent likelihood of a victory by Hillary Clinton. The findings lacked validity and statistical tools were not reliable. What happened?
Answer:
   The polls failed to catch the actual voting patterns that occurred in nine states where Hillary Clinton and Donald Trump were running neck and neck.

Pollsters had complete data but deception and intensity apparently made it invalid and unreliable.

UNDERLYING FACTORS AND BIAS

Research is often performed to confirm a viewpoint. The element of bias needs to be particularly avoided.

- Conscious Bias. A prejudgment that interferes with an objective perspective. Some people like something. Others dislike it.
- Subconscious Influence. Hidden ideas, wishes or desires, traumatic memories, or painful emotions are subconscious influences that affect scholarly research. There may not be much we can do about this.

Question:
   Did voter bias play a role in the U.S. presidential election in 2016?
Answer:
   Unreliable responses may have occurred from hidden biases:

- Nonresponse Bias. Maybe more Trump voters simply didn't answer the phone.
- Social Desirability Bias. Candidate Trump's controversial comments at campaign rallies may have caused individuals to lie to pollsters.
- Emotional Bias. Maybe the polls did not capture the intensity of support for the candidates. High levels of anger and low favorable views from the electorate may have produced an ambivalence that caused voters to stay home. Late developing unfriendly media coverage may have been a factor.

CONCLUSION

Identifying data and converting it into an understanding of causal and correlated relationships is a component of the process of dealing with variables. Done right, it pursues validity and reliability and produces valuable information and then knowledge.

NOTES

1. Michael Lewis, "No-Stats All Star," *New York Times*, February 13, 2009)
2. Shane Battier data is from Malcolm Gladwell, *Blink: The Power of Thinking without Thinking* (New York: Little, Brown and Company, 2005).
3. Team records data from Gladwell, *Blink*.

Chapter Ten

Where Can You Find Hints and Tips for Writing a Dissertation? Don't You Want to Do It Right the First Time?

If you can't do the little things right, you will never do the big things right.
—William H. McRaven, Admiral in the U.S. Navy

REFERENCE BOOKS ON WRITING DISSERTATIONS

It's a simple trip to Amazon Books to find help on writing a dissertation.

Question:
  What's the first book a prospective doctoral candidate should read?
Answer:
  According to its authors, the book should be *Writing the Doctoral Dissertation: A Systematic Approach* by Davis, Parker, and Straub (Barron's). It covers selecting a topic, advisor, and dissertation committee and managing the process of researching, writing, and finishing.
  The Davis et al. book suggests a timetable for writing the dissertation, as shown in table 10.1.

Question:
  Where can you find forms to speed up the process of writing a dissertation?
Answer:
  In the 2006 book *Complete Your Dissertation or Thesis in Two Semesters or Less* by Evelyn Ogden (Lanham, MD: Rowman & Littlefield). It helps make the writing process more efficient.

Table 10.1.

Activity	Months	Percent of Time
Writing, editing, and proofing	5	33%
Research and analysis	7	47%
Review of literature	1	7%
Topic analysis and proposal	2	13%
		100%

Source: Gordon B. Davis, Clyde A. Parker, and Detmar W. Straub, *Writing the Doctoral Dissertation: A Systematic Approach* (Hauppauge, NY: Barron's Educational Service, Inc., 1979).

Question:
Where can you find a book with wisdom, humor, and wonderful practicality to help with your dissertation?
Answer:
The author thinks you already found it because you are reading this book. If it's not enough, try *Writing Your Dissertation in Fifteen Minutes a Day* by Joan Bolker (Henry Holt and Company). This is a guide to starting, revising, and finishing a dissertation.

COMMON QUESTIONS ON WRITING DISSERTATIONS

Let's explore some tips and tricks.

Question:
How long should a dissertation be?
Answer:
Do not expect this question to be answered other than "long enough to achieve high quality standards."

- Literature Review. Four to six categories of scholarly works that bring you to a current significant topic.
- Research Discussion. Complete effort on four to six issues (hypotheses?) explaining what was done and what it means.
- Findings. Complete coverage of significance, limitations, and areas for further research.
- Format. Adequate introduction, abstract, tables, and bibliography.

Question:

Will your advisor read the whole dissertation?

Answer:
You hope the answer is no. If you develop the advisor's confidence that you are doing serious work, the advisor does not need to read the entire document. As an anecdotal observation, some advisors will do so. Most will not.

Question:
How does a school match a candidate and advisor?
Answer:
Don't ask. Instead learn how to influence the process. Learn the politics of the doctoral program. Figure out reality as opposed to mythology.

Question:
Once I know the process, what do I do?
Answer:
Master the task of finding the right advisor. Identify key faculty members who are the decision makers. Build relationships with them. Select the pool of possible advisors and get one or more of them on board. Keep at it until you have the right advisor.

Question:
What makes a good faculty advisor for a dissertation project?
Answer:
Pretty simple: qualified to help you with the topic and methodology, wants to help you, and likes you.

Question:
Who approves topics, proposals, drafts, and final documents?
Answer:
It depends on the university setup. Some structures include:

- Advisor plus Second Reader. One person to coach the candidate and another to confirm standards are met.
- Advisor plus Doctoral Committee Members. One coach and all dissertations reviewed by a committee.
- Advisor plus Outside Defense Panel. One coach plus reviewers selected from the field of study or methodology experts.

Chapter 10
REDUNDANCY

The term "redundancy" deserves a serious look at the start of the dissertation process. Redundancy can be good:

> Redundancy: The inclusion of extra components that are not strictly necessary but support other features and reduce the chance of failure.

Or bad:

> Redundancy. The inclusion of components that are neither needed or useful.

Or descriptive:

> Redundancy. The use of words or data that can be omitted without loss of meaning or function but simply serve as repetition or superfluous information that serves no useful purpose.

Question:
Is redundancy good or bad in a doctoral dissertation?
Answer:
It can be either. Some advisors expect lengthy documents even though the document would be improved by sharper focuses in the methodology, findings, limitations, and further research.

Question:
Where is the best place for redundancy if that is the expectation of the doctoral program or the advisor?
Answer:
The literature review is usually quite safe. Consider which of the following is preferable. It is largely a matter of how much you value redundancy.

Basic Citation. Hogan and Holland (2003) contended that meta-analytical reviews have demonstrated that personality measures are "useful predictors of job performance." Hogan and Shelton (1998) also demonstrated that well-constructed personality measures could predict occupational performance.

Added to the Citation as Redundancy. Personality is often defined in terms of trait theory (Hogan & Shelton, 1998) and the five-factor model (FFM) consisting of emotional stability, extraversion-ambition, agreeableness, conscientiousness, and intellect-openness (Hogan & Holland, 2003).

Question:
What's the role of violence for the doctoral candidate writing a dissertation?
Answer:

It is an unpleasant emotion or destructive natural force, as when candidate must repeat a tedious effort for no reason other than pure stupidity.

Question:
What's an example of dissertation violence?
Answer:
How about this Internet post in 2011?[1]

> I "lost" my thesis today, at around 12:42 pm (thesis RIP). Microsoft word couldn't cope with the size of the document and my file got corrupted. I have a backup from yesterday so I only lost one full day's work.... Hey ho, not the end of the world. Back your work up, I can't possibly imagine what would have happened if I'd really lost everything weeks before submission.

Or this:

> In the spring of 1936, Edna St. Vincent Millay largely completed a play and left the document at home while she went on vacation. When the Palms Hotel caught fire, and burned to the ground, her manuscript was destroyed. She rewrote it from memory and it was published in 1937.[2]

Question:
In today's modern technology, candidates know to back up their dissertations. Thus they avoid one dissertation violence. Is there any likely violence that is frequent?
Answer:
Yes. The most common occurs during the literature review. Let's take a look.

CITATION

A citation is a quotation from or reference to a book, paper, or author, especially in a scholarly work. It allows a researcher to identify information without threat of plagiarism and adds credibility to the effort by assigning proper authority to a statement. In most writing, authors have leeway with the style of literature citation. This is not the case for dissertations. Candidates must follow specific styles:

- In-Text Citations. Usually consists of the author(s) last name(s) and the year of publication.
- Literature Citations. Requires complete references in specified formats. They may be organized in alphabetical order or by website title or URL

with date of publication, article title, journal or magazine title (written in italics), year of publication, and page numbers.

Question:
   Where is the violence with citations?
Answer:
   It lies in the redundancy of repeating the process of finding references and listing them according to the required format when the list has fifty or more citations. This occurs when the research is casual during the period when the candidate is choosing a topic. The citation is missing information. Later, when it's needed in the literature review, the candidate wastes time tracking it down and revising it.

The candidate avoids the violence of citation redundancy by keeping a format sheet handy and perfecting every citation as it is reviewed. Examples include:

- Journal Article. Alstrom, C., R. Blanchard, D. Garcia, and J. Lopez. 2015. Reflections on Duopolies in Financial Markets. *Investment Management* 53: 645–663.
- Book. Lufkin, C. A., and R. Daniels. 2006. *Topology of Southern China.* Florida State University Press, Tallahassee, FL.
- In a Book. Lawrence, S. P., and T. A. Harris. 1999. Corrosive Projects. In: Lang, E. A. (ed.) *Engineering*, vol. 2. ABC Press, Tampa, FL, pp. 141–148.
- Website. Humanistic Society of Canada. October 24, 2014. Statement on MMOs. http://humanistic.org/mmo (no author or publication date so citation date is used).
- Website. Jenkins, P. 2013. Extraneous Isomorphs. http://dynamic organisms.com/22454 (with author and date).

You can help avoid citation violence by keeping a log and meticulously documenting a source when you find it.

PREPROPOSAL STATEMENT

A brief presentation of the concept of a dissertation includes major elements such as a topic, title, purpose, significance, research methodology, limitations, hypotheses, and structure of the literature review. Some examples are discussed here.

Preproposal: A Dissertation on Economic Development

Title. Management Practices in Banking and Insurance: Case Study Energy Sector in Qatar

Purpose. To examine the current view of professionals with respect to factors that encourage or impede the development of conventional and Takaful insurance products to support the global needs of the financial and energy sectors of Qatar.

Significance. The study will contribute to the body of knowledge in Takaful and other risk transfer methods in the emerging Qatari energy and financial markets.

Research Methodology. The primary research will use a mixed-method (quantitative and qualitative) design with a questionnaire creating data on business practices. Target sample size is ten to twenty finance and insurance company professionals completing written questionnaires. Survey findings to be shared with four to six senior business executives with their views recorded, synthesized, and contrasted.

Research Questions (RQ)

RQ1. How do senior staff and employees of Qatari conventional and Islamic banks and insurance firms describe their decision-making processes, pertaining to knowledge management and intellectual capital practices used to improve firm performance?

RQ2. How do senior staff and employees in Qatari banks and insurance firms decide to use knowledge management and intellectual capital practices to improve firm performance?

RQ3. What are the experiences of Qatari insurance firm staff, pertaining to human capital, structural capital, and relational capital?

Structure of the Literature Review

Divided into four topical areas:

- Islamic banking and Takaful insurance
- Conventional banking and insurance in Qatar
- Insurance needs of the energy sector in Qatar
- Capabilities of Qatari financial sector to meet energy sector needs

Preproposal: A Dissertation on Leadership

Title. Perception of Barriers to Advancement of Female Professionals: Case Study Botswana 2016

Purpose. To examine the current view of professionals with respect to the factors that influence whether professional women in Botswana have the prospect to achieve holistic total leadership growth within the G = RH4 model discussed in the literature review. The perspectives will be validated and/or refuted by seasoned executives chosen from the Botswanan business sector.

Significance. The study will contribute to leadership theory by expanding our understanding of the expectations and perceived performance of women in a modern emerging market at a fixed moment in time.

Research Methodology. A mixed-method (quantitative and qualitative) design with a questionnaire seeking perceptions on teamwork, leadership skills, educational achievement, threats from ambitious females, trust considerations, criticism of subordinates, and fears of failure.

- Target sample size is 80 to 100 useful completed questionnaires.
- Target experts are four to six selected by the researcher.
- Likert scale findings will be shared with the experts and their views synthesized and contrasted.

Hypotheses

1. Working on Teams.
    Hypo: Males do not want to work on teams led by females.
    Hypo: Females do not want to work on teams led by females.
2. Threat from Ambitious Females
    Hypo: Males do not respect females who are ambitious.
    Hypo: Females do not respect other females who are ambitious.
3. Lack of Trust
    Hypo: Males do not trust females as bosses.
    Hypo: Females do not trust females as bosses.
4. Acceptance of Feedback
    Hypo: Males have more difficulty accepting criticism from females than from males.
    Hypo: Females have more difficulty accepting criticism from females than from males.

Preproposal: A Dissertation on Management

Title. Perspectives on Staff Knowledge, Skills, and Attitudes in Care for Aging Patients in Institutional Settings

Purpose of the Study. To assess the perspectives of experienced medical and nonmedical personnel on how to develop the proper knowledge, skills, and attitudes (KSAs) for taking care of older adults in institutional settings.

Significance. To contribute to the body of knowledge in geriatric medicine by improving care and reducing costs.

Research Methodology. A mixed-method (quantitative and qualitative) design. Target sample size is ten to twenty experienced health care providers in geriatric facilities. Survey findings shared with four to six senior executives with their views synthesized and contrasted.

Findings Sought

1. What knowledge is weak or missing in new health care providers when they complete community college health professions programs?

2. What skills are missing in new health care providers when they complete community college health professions programs?

3. What attitudes need to be present in interviews with new health care providers when they apply for jobs after completing community college health professions programs?

4. How satisfied are senior staff and medical providers with health care providers in the first year of on-the-job training in institutional settings?

Structure of the Literature Review

Four topical areas:

- Community college preparation for students in health care professions programs
- Knowledge needed for caring for older residents in institutional settings
- Scholarly models for providing or improving geriatric services in institutional settings
- Scholarly research on the needs of the aging

INCORPORATING THE ADVISOR

A second suggestion is to discuss with an advisor a topic early in its formation. This can reduce the redundancies that occur with multiple proposals. Examples follow.

Advisor Discussion: Compensation as a Motivator

Candidate. I am looking forward to working with you. I want to compare the major theories of leadership and confirm or refute the linkage between compensation and job satisfaction.

Director. It sounds pretty broad. What do you know about compensation?

Candidate. The most compelling research is a meta-analysis by Tim Judge et al. The authors reviewed 120 years of research to synthesize the findings from ninety-two quantitative studies. The combined dataset included over 15,000 individuals and 115 correlation coefficients.

Director. What did they find?

Candidate. Results indicate that the association between salary and job satisfaction is very weak. The reported correlation (r = .14) indicates that there is less than 2 percent overlap between pay and job satisfaction levels. Furthermore, the correlation between pay and pay satisfaction was only marginally higher (r = .22 or 4.8 percent overlap), indicating that people's satisfaction with their salary is mostly independent of their actual salary.

Director. Did they create a recognized theory on compensation?

Candidate. Sort of, but the world has changed. In an age of billionaires everybody wants money. My research will show money to correlate much more closely with satisfaction on the job.

Director. I reviewed your proposal. I think it's too broad. Would you consider revising it?

Candidate. Of course.

Director. You are proposing a descriptive dissertation that will be implied in your review of the literature. What is the primary research?

Candidate. I could get compensation data from organizations and compare it with employee turnover and retention as valid measurements of satisfaction.

Director. Do you realize the difficulty of isolating compensation as the independent variable?

Candidate. I could survey people and limit my findings to perceptions.

Director. That would work. What would you ask them?

Candidate. Is the level of pay correlated to job satisfaction in your workplace?

Director. Do you think it would be tricky to validate their answers?

Candidate. I could ask them to identify the evidence they see to justify their answers.

Director. Isn't that kind of anecdotal?

Candidate. I want to refute the research that money does not motivate people.

Director. Isn't that a different issue?

Candidate. In my last job, the company fired one of its best workers because he complained about his low salary. I want to know why.

Director. What does that have to do with your dissertation?

Candidate. I want to correct a lack of understanding of the role of compensation.

Director. Is a series of interviews enough evidence to draw valid conclusions?

Candidate. What do you suggest?

Director. Separate the "crusading" from the primary research. Move on. Find a topic that fits the model of testing independent and dependent variables, correlating them, and determining causation.

Candidate. Are you rejecting my proposal?

Director. You got it.

Advisor Discussion: Loyalty and Link to Performance

Candidate. I would like to develop a theory on the role of loyalty in organizations.

Director. What method would you use?

Candidate. Grounded theory. An inductive approach in which raw data is combined to create a theoretical perspective.

Director. How would it work?

Candidate. I would interview ten to twenty managers in four main areas: their background and demographic, work experience, opinions about loyalty, and knowledge of loyalty. Computer software would convert the transcripts of the oral interviews into text and data would be coded and organized to identify key terms. The frequency and severity of terms would allow abstraction into a new theoretical perspective of the role of loyalty in organizations.

Director. Well, that sounds interesting. The findings would also be significant for subsequent research in management and leadership

CONCLUSION

The books on writing a dissertation and the tips that come from them are useful. They should be compared to the guidance from the school awarding the degree to enhance efforts to complete a successful research project. Then the candidate makes sense out of what's recommended and chooses the path to go forward.

NOTES

1. Post from http://ask.metafilter.com/270272/Dissertation-panic-how-can-I-get-through-the-last-two-days.
2. Source: https://www.poetryfoundation.org/poets/edna-st-vincent-millay.

Chapter Eleven

Do Scholarly Researchers Have Their Own Language? Where Is a Translator When We Need One?

> The limit of my language is the limit of my world.
> —Ludwig Wittgenstein, Austrian-British philosopher

TIME IN RESEARCH

Time is an important factor in any research design. Two major distinctions include:

- Cross-Sectional Study. Happens at a moment in time.
- Longitudinal Study. Repeated observations of the same variables over a period of time.

Question:
   A research study looks at differences in the perception of parents and grandparents with respect to teaching ethical behavior to high school students. The findings contrast the views of the two groups. Is this a cross-sectional or longitudinal study?
Answer:
   We need more information. Is it the perception of what's happening in schools today, what happened when the respondents were in school themselves, or some other structure of the time period?

Question:

Does a relationship exist between a person's income and the amount of usage of Uber for transportation in Manhattan, New York, in 2017? This kind of study is an example of which of the following?

- Cross-sectional analysis
- Longitudinal analysis
- Causal analysis
- Quantitative analysis

Answer:
Cross-sectional analysis.

Question:
Do hedge fund managers adjust the balance of holdings of debt and equity investments based on changes in the Federal Reserve Discount Rate? This is an example of which of the following?

- Cross-sectional analysis
- Longitudinal analysis
- Causal analysis
- Quantitative analysis

Answer:
Longitudinal analysis.

Question:
Does a relationship exist between an Ivy League doctoral degree and success achieving tenure in a college or university? This kind of study is an example of which of the following?

- Cross-sectional analysis
- Longitudinal analysis
- Qualitative analysis
- Quantitative analysis

Answer:
It can be any of them, depending on the research design.

HYPOTHESIS

This is a tentative assumption made in order to test its logical or empirical consequences. It can be a theory, idea, or explanation that will be tested by scholarly research. It is more than a wild guess but less than a well-established theory. It often compares variables:

- Directional Hypothesis. Specifies the relationship between an independent and dependent variable.
- Nondirectional Hypothesis. It compares two variables when neither one is identified as independent or dependent.

The pattern of relationship between two variables can be positive or negative. It can be linear or curvilinear. It can be no relationship at all. The relationship can be tested positive or negative:

- Alternative Hypothesis. A relationship exists between variables X and Y.
- Null Hypothesis. No relationship exists between the variables.

Hypotheses tested by statistical methods can be expressed as one-tailed or two-tailed.

- One-Tail Hypothesis. The mean is significantly greater than or less than X but not both.
- Two-Tail Hypothesis. The critical area of a distribution is greater than or less than a certain range of values.

Question:
A researcher believes children have a higher IQ if they eat fish rich in omega-3 fatty acids. What are alternative and null hypothesis for such an experiment?
Answer:

- Alternative Hypothesis. Children who eat omega-3 fatty acid fish for one year will increase their score on an IQ test by more than children who did not.
- Null Hypothesis. Children who do not eat omega-3 fatty acid fish for one year will not decrease their score on an IQ test by more than children who did.

DIALOGUE ON RESEARCH METHODOLOGY

All of these issues come together as components of the methodology for conducting research. A director can help a candidate choose methodology that matches a research effort.

Candidate. I would like to develop a theory on the role of loyalty in organizations.

Director. What method would you use?

Candidate. Grounded theory. An inductive approach in which raw data is combined to create a theoretical perspective.

Director. How would it work?

Candidate. I would interview ten to twenty managers in four main areas: their background and demographics, work experience, opinions about loyalty, and knowledge of loyalty. Computer software would convert the transcripts into data to be coded by key terms. The frequency and severity of terms would allow abstraction into a new theoretical perspective of the role of loyalty in organizations.

Director. Well, that sounds interesting. The findings would also be significant for subsequent research in management and leadership.

COHORT STUDY

This is a common research design that compares and analyzes people. Key terms are:

- Cohort. A group of individuals who share a common characteristic or experience.
- Control Group. Another group of individuals who do not share the common characteristic.
- Case Control. Analyzes individuals with a common experience compared with individuals who do not share that experience.
- Prospective Study. A longitudinal cohort study that selects a characteristic of a cohort and control group and watches over time to identify differences in outcomes.
- Retrospective Study. A longitudinal cohort study that follows cohorts and the control group over time and compares an outcome.

Question:
A research study will compare the careers of last year's graduates of a private high school and all public high schools in terms of future career success. What kind of study is this?
Answer:
A longitudinal, prospective, cohort study.

Question:
A research study compared the careers of 1985 graduates of a public and private high school and evaluated which school produced the most successful individuals. What kind of study is this?
Answer:
A longitudinal, retrospective, cohort study.

Question:
In the study of 1985 graduates, which group is the control group?
Answer:
We don't know. If the study compared one school with all 1985 high school graduates, the individual school would clearly be the cohort. With two schools, it depends on the definitions of the researcher.

Question:
A research statement is "Do ten current professors, five of whom received tenure and five who were denied tenure, agree that loyalty is a factor that affects performance?" Is this a cohort or case-control research statement?
Answer:
Both.

Question:
Is the previous statement cross-sectional or longitudinal?
Answer:
It depends on whether tenure decisions all occurred at the same time.

DESCRIPTIVE STUDY

This research describes characteristics of a population or phenomenon. It does not answer questions about what caused a situation. As a result, descriptive research has a lower level of validity than is generally expected of scholarly research.

Question:
A dissertation proposal seeks to explain the structure of the worldwide coal mining industry, the working conditions of coal miners, and the attitudes of government agencies and executives who manage coal companies. Is this a viable topic for a dissertation?
Answer:
Not likely. It could be at least three separate dissertations.

EXPERIMENTAL STUDY

This occurs when a procedure or behavior is intentionally undertaken and a result or outcome is observed. In human experiments, the study has three elements:

- Manipulation. The researcher gives the subjects a stimulus and observes the reaction or response.
- Control. The procedure is repeatable under identical conditions with multiple subjects.
- Random Selection and Assignment. Participants in a sample are selected and assigned to the study and control groups on a random basis.

Question:
   A research experiment measures the preference of adults for three different advertising flyers. One flyer is shown in a wealthy section of town, another in a poor section, and the third to residents of nursing homes. Statistically, the poor section residents gave the flyer the highest scores. What's the level of validity and reliability of this experimental study?
Answer:
   It might meet the manipulation and control requirements but violates random selection and assignment. It is neither valid nor reliable in a comparison study.

Question:
   Does the study of advertising flyers have any validity or reliability at all?
Answer:
   Maybe. Its only validity comes from a preference if used solely in each of the target economic communities.

RESEARCH FALLACY

A fallacy is an error in a premise, reasoning, or logic. Two categories include:

- Induction Fallacy. Draw a conclusion on an individual based on analysis of a group.
- Deduction Fallacy. Draw a conclusion on a group based on analysis from a single case.

Question:
   Everybody knows economics majors have the highest grade point average of any academic program. Joe is an economics major. Is he an A student?

Answer:
We don't know. Induction fallacy, if we claim to know.

Question:
A woman is driving a car when another driver swerves in front of her. She hits the brakes too hard and causes an accident. Is this a sign that women are terrible drivers?

Answer:
We don't know. Deduction fallacy, if we believe it.

CONCLUSION

A simple listing of various research terms shows the depth and breadth of scholarly research. A doctoral candidate or professor can choose from qualitative or quantitative, deductive or inductive, theoretical or empirical, descriptive or experimental, and more to search for new knowledge.

Chapter Twelve

Does a Quantitative or Qualitative Dissertation Make More Sense? Do You Want to Know the Answer Now or After You Attempt It?

> I abhor averages. A man may have six meals one day and then none the next making an average of three meals a day but that is not a good way to live.
> —Louis D. Brandeis, U.S. Supreme Court Justice

Question:
   An economist was testifying as an expert witness in a wrongful termination lawsuit. A female assistant professor had been denied promotion and tenure. Her allegation was gender discrimination. Data showed the university advanced 73 percent of males and 70 percent of females over a fifteen-year period. The expert said the data showed a pattern of discrimination. How did he explain it?

Answer:
   He could not explain it. He simply said repeatedly that he ran a complex statistical algorithm and it showed discrimination. The small differential between 73 and 70 percent did not matter. The statistical calculation was more accurate.

STATISTICS AND PURPOSIVE SAMPLING

Statistics is the science of collecting, analyzing, and making inference from data. It's a practical approach to scientific inquiry about causal and correlated relationships. Purposive sampling gives us data. Statistics gives us tools. Where would we be without probability of the likelihood of an occurrence?

Statistical analysis supports logic and evidence-based reasoning. Tests for statistical significance provide evidence to confirm or refute hypotheses.

DESCRIPTIVE STATISTICS AND STATISTICAL INFERENCE

Two approaches to using statistics are used to draw conclusions on a population:

- Descriptive Statistics. When we have data on the entire population.
- Statistical Inference. When we have data from a sample.

Purposive sampling, also known as judgmental, selective, or subjective sampling, uses statistical inference to understand the relationships of variables.

Question:
 Eighty percent of the entering freshmen at a large university had a test score that placed them in the top quartile of high school students. Is this a descriptive statistic or statistical inference?
Answer:
 Descriptive statistic. Inference is not required because the data describe a total population, not a sample.

Question:
 Based on data collected from twenty-four universities, a researcher determined that 70 percent of college freshmen had a test score that placed them in the top quartile of high school students. Is this a descriptive statistic or statistical inference?
Answer:
 Statistical inference, as the finding did not include data from all high school students.

SIGNIFICANCE DEFINED

A researcher claims to have statistical significance from data. What does that mean? Two possibilities include:

- Significant in Research. A finding is sufficiently important because it adds to our knowledge in a specialized field.
- Statistical Significance. A finding explains a likely relationship between two or more variables is caused by something other than random chance.

Question:
A research study claims a 95 percent likelihood that 45 percent of a company's employees like their boss. The margin of error is 4 percent. What's the level of statistical significance?
Answer:
We expect 95 percent of the total values to be within the range of 41 to 49 percent.

Question:
A professor wants to know the average age of every student in her class. She obtains from the registrar the birth dates of all thirty students and calculates 20.6 years as the average age. What's the level of likely error for the study?
Answer:
Zero. Absent errors in data entry, no error exists because she has the entire population.

CORRELATION AND CAUSATION

Dependence or association is any statistical relationship. Choices include:

- Correlation. A relationship useful for understanding or predicting.
- Causation. A relationship linking an independent and dependent variable.

Question:
Over a ten-year period, a country experienced a 3.5 percent rise in inflation. During the same period, doctors reported a 3.5 percent rise in heart attacks. It appears that inflation endangers people's health. Do you agree?
Answer:
No. Correlation is not causation.

Question:
The average July temperature in a country is 80° Fahrenheit (27° Celsius). Above that, every 5 percent rise in temperature causes a 7 percent rise in electricity usage. It appears that electricity usage causes a rise in temperature. Do you agree?
Answer:
No, but the opposite may be true. With an evaluation of the availability of air conditioning in the country, causation may be producing correlation.

Correlation may imply causation but care must be taken when drawing conclusions from the data.

Chapter 12

CORRELATION MEASURES

Statistical efforts to link variables include:

- Correlation Coefficient. Denoted ρ or r, this measures the degree of correlation. The Pearson correlation coefficient is a measure of the linear correlation between two variables X and Y. Total positive correlation is one, no correlation is zero, and total negative correlation is minus one.
- Coefficient of Determination. Denoted R^2 (R squared), this is the proportion of the variance in the dependent variable that is predictable from the independent variable(s).
- Coefficient of Multiple Correlation. Denoted R, this is a measure of how well other variables predict an outcome in a linear relationship.

Question:
  Are nonlinear or other more sophisticated correlation measures available to link independent and dependent variables?
Answer:
  Yes, for example, Spearman's rank correlation, Kendall tau rank correlation, distance correlation, randomized dependence correlation, multimoment correlation, and polychoric correlation.

CASE STUDY: STATISTICAL SIGNIFICANCE

Statistics give researchers a powerful tool. No question about it. At the same time, heavy statistical analysis complicates the massive research often undertaken with doctoral dissertations.

As an example, consider actual data used in a dissertation on loyalty in organizations. The research starts with a goal:

Goal

To compare the relationship between perceived loyalty by bosses and employees and the level of organizational revenues and employee satisfaction.

The researcher developed hypotheses:

Hypotheses

- H1: The higher the level of perceived loyalty by the employee, the higher the level of revenues.
- H2: The higher the level of perceived loyalty by the boss, the higher the level of revenues.

- H3: The higher the level of perceived loyalty by the employee, the higher the level of employee satisfaction.
- H4: The higher the level of perceived loyalty by the boss, the higher the level of employee satisfaction.

Using written responses from a sample of more than two hundred individuals, the findings were presented based on multiple regression analysis.

Findings

- H1. The positive beta coefficient sign ($\beta = .529$) of the loyalty variable suggests that revenues will increase by .529 units for every unit increase in loyalty from the boss. This confirms the first hypothesis.
- H2. The positive beta coefficient sign ($\beta = .453$) suggests that revenues will increase by .453 units for every unit increase in loyalty perceived by the boss. This confirms the second hypothesis.
- H3. The positive sign of the beta coefficient of the interaction term ($\beta = .188$) suggests that high loyalty perceived by the employee increases employee satisfaction by .188. This confirms the third hypothesis.
- H4. The positive sign of the beta coefficient of the interaction term ($\beta = .163$) suggests that the perception of loyalty by the boss increases employee satisfaction by .163. This confirms the fourth hypothesis.

The backup mathematical data was many pages in length.

Question:
 Is the regression in the case study a valid scholarly research effort?
Answer:
 Of course. Using a widely recognized statistical approach, it evaluated the relationship among variables and confirms hypotheses with respect to them.

Question:
 Did it provide valid findings with respect to the role of loyalty in the workplace?
Answer:
 If it's free of errors, it offers valid findings. When a doctoral candidate conducts a quantitative study, the effort must be valid in terms of the statistical tools as well as the research methodology employed.

Question:
 All looks in order for a solid statistical dissertation. So what's the danger of doing it?
Answer:

Statistics pose a problem to move a dissertation along through the process of approval. Every new submission takes time to analyze by the director or other approving parties. The effort can bog down with big delays.

BEWARE THE COMPLEXITY OF THE STATISTICS

The message from the case study may or may not be clear. Let's make it explicit. If you tackle a highly complex statistical project, recognize the possibility that it will take a long time or a little luck to move it through the approval process.

The following true story reinforces this message, albeit with a positive outcome.

CASE STUDY: RESOLVING STATISTICAL VALIDITY

An American university agreed to provide financial support for the pursuit of a doctoral degree. The understanding was that success would move the woman from a lecturer to assistant professor on a tenure-track line. She completed the doctoral course work and written exams, reaching the all-but-dissertation (ABD) stage.

She canvassed the professors in her department and discovered that none would serve as her dissertation director. One offered to accept the duty if she took an unpaid leave of absence from her teaching position and worked for a year as his graduate assistant. She could not afford to make this sacrifice.

Her home university had an exchange agreement with a Chinese university. The two schools arranged for her to teach in China while she wrote a dissertation. Ostensibly it would be supervised by a Chinese professor.

As she progressed, she had no help as the Chinese professors seemed to avoid her. She turned in her dissertation and requested a date for the oral examination. Nothing happened for months.

She appealed to the president of her home university. The president asked for a copy of the dissertation and gave it to a faculty member who verified the soundness of the statistics used to manipulate the data and produce the findings. The president then emailed the president of the Chinese university but received no explanation for the delay.

It was nearing the end of the candidate's time in China and she faced the prospect of leaving without defending the document. Panic was setting in.

The president of the American school went to China on a routine visit. He met with the Chinese president and explained that more delay would disrupt the friendly relations between the two universities. He pleaded for help.

Question:

Did the candidate get help obtaining approval for an oral defense?
Answer:
Yes. Unexpectedly, a Chinese professor scheduled the oral examination and the candidate received the degree. Guanxi, the Chinese concept of support relationships and cooperation, between the two presidents triumphed over the problem.

Question:
Did the Chinese professor ever explain the delay?
Answer:
Yes. At the start of the oral defense, a Chinese professor apologized for the delay. He explained the American approach to the statistics was not understood by the Chinese professors. Out of respect for their American colleagues, they accepted an American professor's certification that the statistics were sound and voted to schedule the defense and then approve the degree.

Question:
What's the lesson learned from the story of the Chinese dissertation?
Answer:
A doctoral candidate should try to develop strong advocacy and support from powerful faculty members as a hedge against unforeseen obstacles to completing the dissertation. This is particularly the case with heavy statistical projects.

CONCLUSION

The role of statistics is sizeable in modern research and the statistical tools have expanded exponentially with advances in computer and other technology. Still, researchers must ensure that they have a complete understanding of the mathematical aspects of research prior to undertaking a quantitative dissertation or similar research project. Dissertation candidates must also be aware of built-in dangers when professors who must approve a dissertation bog down in the task of validating it.

Chapter Thirteen

How Does Sampling Produce Valid Findings? Does Anybody Believe What We Learned?

> There are three kinds of lies: lies, damned lies, and statistics.
> —Popularized by Mark Twain, American author, and attributed to Benjamin Disraeli, British Prime Minister

SAMPLING

Sampling refers to the selection of a subset of individuals to estimate characteristics of a whole population. The process has several stages:

- Define the population. Who will be asked questions?
- Specify items to measure. What do we want to know?
- Specify a sampling method. Will it be written or oral?
- Determine the sample size. How many responses will be needed?
- Implement the sampling plan. How will we collect the data?

DEDUCTIVE AND INDUCTIVE RESEARCH

The process of sampling in scholarly research can take either of two directions:

- Deductive. From the theory to the hypothesis to observation to confirmation.
- Inductive. From observation to a pattern to a hypothesis to a theory.

SAMPLING CATEGORIES

Sample categories include:

- Simple Sample. A subset of individuals chosen from a larger set.
- Random Sample. Each individual chosen randomly and entirely by chance. Every individual in the population has the same probability of being chosen.
- Convenience or Quota Sample. Choose randomly among subjects or data that are readily available. Sometimes called accidental or haphazard sampling.

POPULATION OF SAMPLE GROUP

We can identify two approaches to selecting individuals or data in a sample:

- Homogeneous. Members or units are similar. The goal of the research is to understand a particular group in depth.
- Heterogeneous. Members or units are diverse in character or content. The goal of the research does not focus on a single uniform group.

Question:
  Two hundred people at a protest rally were asked if they drink Pepsi. Thirty-five percent said yes. What does this tell us about the percentage of people in the country who drink Pepsi?
Answer:
  Not much.

RANDOM SAMPLE

A random sample is a subset of a population chosen entirely by chance. Each individual or data item has the same probability of being chosen. Types of random samples include:

- Simple. Choose anyone or any data in a population. All individuals between the ages of thirty-one and forty.
- Systematic. Line up the subjects or data and count off "1, 2, 3, 4; 1, 2, 3, 4." When done, choose all data with the number two.
- Stratified. Divide the population into homogeneous subgroups. Only college graduates between the ages of thirty-one and forty.

USING SAMPLES IN RESEARCH

Statistical sampling leads to generalizations with calculated degrees of certainty. Random and quota samples are both used. Only a true random sample has sufficient validity and reliability to meet many research standards. Quota samples are valuable so long as we recognize their limitations in terms of statistical accuracy.

PROBABILITY AND NONPROBABILITY SAMPLES

A probability sample exists when every subject or item of data has the same chance to be selected. A nonprobability sample exists when some subjects or data items are excluded. A simple, systematic, or stratified random sample can be either probability or nonprobability. A convenience or quota sample is always nonprobability.

We can compare features of probability and nonprobability samples, as shown in table 13.1.

STATISTICALLY SIGNIFICANT

This is the likelihood that a relationship between two or more variables is caused by something other than chance. Determining the level of statistical significance is the goal of statistical hypothesis testing. A test provides a p-value representing the probability that random chance could explain a result. A value of 95 percent means a relationship has a 5 percent or lower chance of being wrong.

Statistical significance is calculated mathematically, with the chi squared test as the most common approach.

Table 13.1.

	Probability	Nonprobability
Basis of Selection	Random	Arbitrary
Research	Conclusive	Exploratory
Result	Unbiased	Biased
Method	Objective	Subjective
Inferences	Statistical	Analytical
Hypothesis	Tested	Generated

CONFIDENCE LEVEL OR INTERVAL

This is the percent of all possible values that can be expected in a population based on a sample of that population. This is the likelihood that the value in the sample is the actual value in the population. A 95 percent confidence level means a sample result has a 95 percent chance of being valid.

Question:
　A researcher said she has a 95 percent level of confidence in the results of the study. How does this differ from the confidence level or interval?
Answer:
　It's the same thing.

T-TEST

An example of a statistical tool is a t-test that determines whether the mean of a population significantly differs from the mean of another population. A t-test is used in random sampling. We can identify dozens if not hundreds of statistical tools in all forms of research. Many of them are built into spreadsheets or available in sophisticated software packages.

Question:
　A researcher wants to produce statistically significant results from a quota sample. How can this be done?
Answer:
　By definition, it can't.

WORD OF CAUTION

Statisticians can be quite rigid on the technical meaning of statistical significance. BASSE researchers also need to be practical. Two important considerations include:

- Sampling Error. The difference between a result obtained from a sample and total population of all individuals or data. Random samples of data or people are not perfect. Subjective factors are always present even though hidden. The selection of people or data can be an imperfect process.
- Probability Is Not Certainty. Statistics is about probability. Scholarly research is about managing risk. What does it cost to increase the probability of improving accuracy from a sample and what are the potential consequences if we are wrong?

Convenience sampling can produce valid and reliable findings but lacks the statistical level of validity and reliability. When all subjects or data are obtainable, researchers should employ probability sampling. When convenience random sampling is employed, the research should not identify a statistical confidence level and point out the use of the quota sample.

Researchers need to be realistic about the greater degree of validity of probability sampling. The argument is made that it is more objective. The decision on what's convenient is subjective. At the same time, sampling almost always involves some level of researcher subjectivity when it involves individual subjects. We can never be sure that everyone who matches a target group is included in the selection of specific individuals.

Nonprobability sampling is not as valid or reliable as probability studies. Many qualified researchers accept its results as valid and reliable when the research is accompanied by an expressed limitation cited in the findings.

Question:
A researcher identified four groups of MBA candidates and divided them into Gen X males, Gen X females, millennial males, and millennial females. He surveyed 120 of them and asked, "On a scale of 1 (least) to 10 (most), what score would you give to nepotism as an act of corruption?" The result was a mean of 7.2 and a median of 5.4. Is this a valid and reliable result?
Answer:
Yes, if the researcher points out the limitation.

Question:
Shaquille O'Neil, basketball player, and Robert Reich, professor and political commentator, have an average height of six feet. What is the statistical significance of this statement?
Answer:
Not much. Robert Reich is 4'10" tall. Shaquille O'Neal is 7'1".

Question:
What sampling method is preferred for dissertation research?
Answer:
If the research project goal is probabilistic forecasting and is going to produce a level of confidence, only a random sample will be accurate.

Question:
A researcher has government data on unemployment in Lebanon, Jordan, Egypt, and the United Arab Emirates. A research project seeks to predict employment trends for the next ten years. Key business leaders will be interviewed. Is this research suitable for a random or quota sampling method?
Answer:

Only a quota sample will work. Problems include:

- Data integrity is not likely given differences in the economic and social conditions in the countries.
- A random sample is nearly impossible to create because respondents may be unable to respond or may decline participation.

USING STATISTICS IN SCHOLARLY RESEARCH

Statistical approaches to extracting meaning and knowledge from ideas, behaviors, and events are highly developed and widely used. They are not appropriate for all studies and must be selected carefully by the researcher.

Question:
　A professor has uncovered a possible relationship that would resolve a controversial argument raging among serious scholars measuring human behavior. The answer to the problem lies in a complicated but apparently valid set of mega data. How should the researcher approach the task of statistically manipulating the data?
Answer:
　The recommendation is "find the most competent statistician or team of statisticians and make them partners in the research."

Question:
　A doctoral candidate has uncovered a possible dissertation topic that requires statistical manipulating of data. What should he do?
Answer:
　See the answer to the previous question. A competent statistician, not the greatest in the world, should be sufficient.

CONCLUSION

Sampling offers a powerful tool for understanding relationships among variables when only a portion of the units of a population are available to researchers. To ensure a reasonable degree of validity and reliability, researchers must exercise care in selecting population and using the right tools to evaluate findings.

Chapter Fourteen

Why Are Limitations as Important as Findings? Do We Need to Explain that which We Didn't Learn?

I have not failed. I've just found 10,000 ways that won't work.
—Thomas A. Edison, inventor, on experiments to find a workable light bulb

RESEARCH LIMITATIONS

Limitations of the dissertation are characteristics of data, design, or methodology that have an impact on the validity of findings. The candidate is expected to acknowledge them. Things to remember include:

- All scholarly research has limitations.
- Recognizing limitations shows the research has critically examined the data, design, and findings.
- In addition to discovering new knowledge, a corollary goal of research is to confront gaps in knowledge.
- A limitation is an opportunity to suggest further research.

As part of the research process, the candidate should be sensitive to certain areas:

- Sample Size. The problem to be investigated determines the number of units of analysis needed to produce valid and reliable findings. In a small sample, statistical results may not produce significant relationships or conclusions.

- Data Availability. The scope of analysis may be limited by a lack of reliable data.
- Absence of Prior Research. The literature review provides the foundation showing you understand the research problem. If prior research is lacking, this is a limitation.
- Methodology. The structure of your primary research can have two kinds of limitations:
- Initial Design. The researcher may not have access to the best tools or information as a result of factors such as cost, legal concerns, or government or university regulations or guidelines.
- Retrospective Knowledge. During the investigation, the researcher may realize a weakness in design or data collection that should be corrected in future research.
- Self-Reported Data. The researcher should distinguish between data provided by individuals or organizations that have a role dealing with the research problem. They may shape events to influence the findings in a positive direction for them. Such data can be used at face value. If the researcher is unable to independently validate key self-reported variables, this is a limitation.
- New Research. After completion of the literature review chapter, the candidate should not be expected to continually update it and use new findings to validate the primary research. If new evidence appears that contradicts the effort, the failure to consider it is a limitation. It rarely should invalidate the effort of a well-designed initial research study.
- Negative Results Can Be Significant. Sometimes the findings do not reveal the relationships as suggested by the literature review. This does not invalidate the dissertation. The absence of confirmation can be a significant finding.

Question:
A research study sought to show a link between family interaction and worsening attention deficit hyperactivity disorder (ADHD) behavior. The findings were inconclusive. Is the study invalid?
Answer:
Not necessarily. As already stated, negative results can point to future research.

Question:
Of the various limitations just listed, which one deserves the most attention from a researcher working on a qualitative research project based on interviews of key people who lived through a crisis?
Answer:

Arguably, the research must beware of the limitations of self-reported data:

- Selective Memory. Remembering or failing to remember experiences or events that occurred at some point in the past.
- Telescoping. Recalling events that occurred at one time as though they occurred at a different time.
- Attribution. Describing one's own actions as producing positive outcomes while attributing negative outcomes to others or external forces.
- Exaggeration. Representing incidents, actions, or events as more significant than they actually were to produce an outcome.

Question:
A candidate evaluated economic conditions in Angola during the period from 1998 to 2002 and drew conclusions on economic developments under extreme wartime conditions. At the oral defense, a committee member said, "A new research study contradicts your interpretation of the role of the National Union for the Total Independence of Angola. What do you think about that?" How should the candidate respond?
Answer:
The candidate should respond that the study would be a fruitful area for further research. If the research is not already identified in the dissertation, the researcher can add its absence to the limitations. Without a thorough evaluation of the new research, the candidate should be comfortable with the dissertation's conclusions.

FORESEEING OBSTACLES: A WORD TO THE WISE

The candidate should consider disruptions at the very start of research design, paying particular attention to:

- Access. If the study depends on obtaining restricted documents, organizational support, or interviews or responses from specific people, ensure access is likely.
- Available Time. Design the project so it can occur in a workable time frame. A dissertation is not the culmination of a lifetime of work.
- Avoid Personal Bias. Do not seek to "prove" something that you intensely believe. Care should be taken to use data as objectively as possible. If the research confirms a strongly held belief, the paper should explain measures taken to be objective.

TIPS ON LIMITATIONS

Some things to consider for limitations:

- Organize Them Together. Limitations of the study should be all in one place. They should not be sprinkled around to mask the scope of them. When pointing out limitations throughout, repeat them in a general listing.
- Flawed Findings. Sometimes findings are unexpectedly seriously flawed. Examples are an inability to acquire critical data or interview key people. If this occurs after considerable research effort, the researcher may be able to reframe the project as an exploratory study that provides the groundwork for a revised effort in the future. If this is the situation, specifically explain the way flaws can be successfully overcome and cite this recommendation as the findings of the dissertation.
- Format for the Limitations. Each important limitation should be individually addressed. Describe it specifically in concise terms.
- Don't Inflate the Importance of Findings. They are what they are. After all the hard work and long hours, the candidate is tempted to assign unwarranted significance to the findings. Avoid this, as it weakens the validity of the effort.
- Insignificant Results Are Not a Limitation. A research effort may not find linkages among relationships as anticipated. Who knew? The research thus may be important to future researchers.

Question:
   A candidate designed a study to interview mayors about a funding problem for local transportation. Halfway through the process, he realized that he would obtain better results interviewing city managers. What should he do?
Answer:
   Acknowledge the situation as a limitation in the completed paper. Explain how interviewing city managers appears to be a more robust methodology.

CONCLUSION

A proper explanation of the limitations of research is an important component of a dissertation. It improves the ability of researchers to understand the validity of findings and uncover likely areas of further research.

III

Candidates Only: Practical Tips for Writing Dissertations

Chapter Fifteen

Why Is a Dissertation like Flying a Fighter Jet? Is It Enough to Take Off or Do You Want to Be Sure You Can Land?

> Writing a dissertation is a lot like running a marathon. They are both endurance events . . . last a long time and . . . require a consistent and carefully calculated amount of effort to complete them and not burn out.
> —*The Dissertation Whisperer*, academic blog

Question:

A candidate received his doctorate from Columbia University. It took a long time. Finally, his advisor said, "I'm signing off on this study. It's arguably the worst dissertation I have ever seen." Did the candidate's efforts produce academic scholarship?

Answer:

Obviously not. This is a true story. The person telling it with a self-deprecating chuckle retired after thirty-five years as a tenured associate professor. He never claimed to be an academic scholar.

THE RIGHT STUFF?

Let's be honest. Under the best of conditions, it's a formidable journey to complete a dissertation. The trek that started with acceptance into a doctoral program takes on a new burden when you achieve ABD status.

Question:
Preparing to enter the weightlessness of space, an astronaut pursues high physical, mental, and emotional standards. He also seeks to develop a firm handshake. Why does he do this?
Answer:
In zero gravity, you don't have much need for your legs. On a spacewalk outside the capsule, repair activities require extraordinary strength in the hands, wrist, and forearms. All the intelligence and mathematics of prior education do not guarantee success without a strong grip on the tools.

Question:
What does weightlessness have to do with a dissertation?
Answer:
Doctoral candidates are rarely prepared for the figurative weightlessness of scholarly research. They float at the end of a tether line hoping to (1) accomplish a task and (2) return safety to the capsule. The astronaut trained in a pool where he learned work while to floating. The doctoral candidate has no such experience. The only hope for success is a strong grip on the research tools. Let's take a look.

THE DISSERTATION AND MOUNT EVEREST

In many ways, writing a dissertation is akin to preparing and then climbing the highest mountain in the world. Training begins years earlier to be in the best possible physical and mental shape. Candidates gather knowledge about the subject and work with experts on strategies to succeed. Once started, the individual is largely alone undertaking a lengthy climb to a revered height. Not everyone makes it. Some quit. Others experience a physical or metaphorical demise.

GETTING A GRIP

A candidate needs to keep moving but should not get carried away with the effort. Choose a topic early after acceptance into the doctoral program. Use coursework to become the world's top expert in a narrow range of investigation. Focus all your energy on a single myopic goal. Complete the dissertation. Relentlessly:

- work closely with the doctoral committee or faculty members who may become mentors or directors.
- prepare a formal proposal and revise it after receiving feedback.

- complete the literature review and bibliography in the style specified by the school.
- perform the primary research.
- develop the findings
- identify areas for future research.
- submit the dissertation.
- participate in an oral defense.

What should you write about? The choice of a workable topic is critical. Some guidelines include:

- Researcher Interest. Pick an area where you have a high level of interest.
- Importance. Deal with some significant issue.
- Prior Scholarly Effort. Ensure the topic has serious prior research shaping it.

Question:
A young man was discussing his acceptance into a doctoral program. It was the fulfillment of a dream. He was asked what was his planned topic for the dissertation. He answered, "I don't know. I will think about that after I finish my coursework and complete the written exams." Is this a good idea?
Answer:
No. This is a very bad idea. With this strategy, the candidate will pay tuition and incur financial costs, suffer lost earnings, and work thousands of hours on assignments that have little value. Make the courses worthwhile by preparing yourself to write a dissertation.

DISSERTATION APPROVALS

Every school has policies covering approvals, formats, and structure.

- Approval of the Proposal. In some programs, you have to propose what you want to do and get approval to do it.
- Format. The dissertation must be formatted according to a style guide, such as APA, Chicago, MLA, and Turabian.
- Structure. The organization of chapters and topics may be spelled out in detail.
- Approval of the Final Document. After completing the dissertation, a remaining step is to obtain acceptance of your work by the dissertation advisor or review panel of professors.

At any point in the process, the journey may end. The candidate may give up or time may run out. The proposal or even the final paper may not be accepted. In any of these situations, the school usually awards a master's degree.

REALITIES OF THE DISSERTATION

The candidate needs to face some issues:

- Review of the Literature. You are reviewing prior research mechanically based on citations often from a distance. To properly understand past research is the task of a lifetime. A review at the start of a career is somewhat shallow as it lacks the perspective that goes with maturity. Accept it for what it is.
- Limited Impact of Findings. The output of the dissertation is usually a set of narrow findings that have minor, if any, impact on the branch of knowledge of the candidate.
- No Focus on Sharing Key Ideas. The value of academic scholarship occurs by sharing critical thought with fellow researchers, students, and thought leaders. Most dissertations do not meet this standard. Most dissertations are never read by other scholars.
- The Process Is Cumbersome. Dissertation guidelines are filled with trivial and almost unbearable requirements that bog down the real pursuit of knowledge. You have to learn how to deal with the situation and keep moving.

FEELING WHEN THE DISSERTATION IS ACCEPTED

The feeling is total exhilaration. It's the same feeling as when you complete Navy Seal Team training, reach the top of Mount Everest, or are released after 20 years in solitary confinement in a maximum-security prison. No doubt about it. Congratulations are in order. It's party time.

BEWARE THE WRONG DISSERTATION DIRECTOR

If you speak to some candidates, the doctoral dissertation is perhaps the cruelest torture ever inflicted upon an unsuspecting human being.

You finished your course work, passed the written exams, and began the final part of a long journey. It does not sound too imposing. Select a topic. Research it. Write it. In reality, it occasionally goes wrong. The most common problem occurs with the failure to choose or be assigned the right faculty director.

Let's be honest. Professors don't have much patience for the work of others. If a doctoral student is not helping with the professor's own research, the professor has little interest in reading a lengthy treatise of a new and perhaps future rival scholar.

A related problem is that many professors have been hardened by their own dissertation process or the subsequent years when their research has not received the acclaim it deserves. They throw obstacles into the way of novitiates seeking a position in the academy. The work of the candidate is never good enough. It is never done.

A candidate should spend considerable time building a relationship with professors who are possibilities to direct the dissertation or to serve on doctoral defense committees.

DISSERTATION STORY (DISGUISED)

Years ago, I wrote a semi-fictional account of a candidate completing a dissertation. It's an amalgamation of stories too often heard in the faculty lounge. Say hello to "Abby Lengren."

Abby chose to research Italian Americans in the early twentieth century. She loved the Godfather movies. Did the Mafia really control the judges, mayors, and U.S. senators? With her attention to detail, she would ferret out the true story of political corruption and write the greatest dissertation ever.

Ah, that was twenty-five months ago. Now, she simply wants to graduate.

For fifteen months, Abby lived in the bowels of the library and ghetto hotels in Chicago, Philadelphia, and New York City. She researched police records and transcripts from trials. She interviewed remarkable, if somewhat cynical, police officers and came to respect them, mostly for the sense of humor that accompanied their work. They knew all the players and current gossip. The research had interesting moments. Soon it would be over.

The process was explained in the Doctoral Student Guide. The candidate would work with a mentor to select a topic, research it, write a dissertation, defend it, and graduate with or without distinction. Sounds organized. Sounds good.

Now it was done. Abby made the copies she would need. 445 pages. Six cents a page. Five copies. 150 dollars. Copies made and distributed to the committee.

Even if she had finished on time, Abby would have been unemployed. Three hundred vitas mailed to academic departments. Sixteen responses. All negative.

As it was, February became June and Abby still had not received comments from three members of the committee. Finally, Professor Sandusky replied:

> I question your research methodology, particularly the interviewing only of police officers. Why did you omit district attorneys and defense lawyers who could give a broader perspective?

That was it. The dreaded death bomb comment. Professor Sandusky did not say "rewrite chapter three, add some sources to your bibliography, or clarify the findings in chapter 14." Any of these comments could be addressed in a few weeks. Interview district attorneys and defense lawyers? More months spent in flea traps in Philadelphia, Chicago, and New York? What would be learned anyway?

In August, Abby got the comments from the final two members of the committee. Only Abrahamson had a comment. He liked the methodology but questioned the finding that the Cosa Nostra was organized like a successful business. He wrote:

> You claim the Cosa Nostra operates like a successful business. This means a profit was made. Why did you omit financial data to support this contention?

Idiot! What did Abrahamson think? The Mafia publishes an annual report and files its financial statements with the Securities and Exchange Commission? Well, at least she could respond. No, the real problem was district attorneys and defense lawyers.

In September, Abby finally got an appointment with Sandusky. He would not budge. Abby spent October to January working part time at odd jobs while meeting with prosecutors and defense attorneys. She rewrote three chapters, made new copies, and finished the job.

It took three months to set a date for the defense, which was a nonevent. Her director, Professor Hintermann, appeared to be distracted. Sandusky controlled the discussion. Abrahamson asked aggressive questions, more to enhance his own reputation rather than to derail a successful defense. The others participated with minor questions.

Professor Marco Pelligrino had one telling observation:

> I don't know why you bothered to interview prosecutors and defense attorneys. Did those interviews really buttress any of your premises or conclusions?

After the committee voted, Abby was invited back into the room and congratulated on a successful defense. She had to make a few minor revisions but she would now be Doctor Lengren. The feeling was every bit as great as she imagined. It was like a mother giving birth to triplets.

Fifteen months to finish the research and write the dissertation. Sixteen more months to set up a successful defense. She finally could leave behind the difficulties of the dissertation from hell.

COMPLETION RATES ON DISSERTATIONS

A chapter in my companion book, *The Professoriate Today: Languishing in Dante's Purgatory*, tells the tale of difficulties finishing a dissertation. It points out that the average time to degree completion ranges from six to eleven years. It identifies obstacles to degree completion including problems with the dissertation director, stress affecting the candidate's health, and misunderstandings that lead to despair. It makes suggestions on how to finish the dissertation as obstacles arise.

REFLECTION

The dissertation is the largest challenge to obtaining recognition as an "expert" in a field. Completing it is an exacting and tedious task in a narrow slice of scholarly activity. A successful result provides a credential and reflects skills and ability to do serious research. Dedication and organization are definitely helpful to completing the project that resembles in one sense a marathon more than a shorter race. In another sense, it's a lonely and weightless space odyssey.

CONCLUSION

No amount of preparation can identify obstacles that arise and slow down or temporarily halt progress with the dissertation. The candidate needs to watch for signs of impending problems and adapt to overcome the difficulties they create.

Chapter Sixteen

What Is the Dilemma of the Dissertation Topic? Why Is It So Important to Resolve It?

> In formal logic, a contradiction is the signal of defeat but in the evolution of real knowledge it marks the first step in progress toward victory.
> —Alfred North Whitehead, philosopher

GREAT SCHOLARSHIP

Some notable research efforts are monumental and would make outstanding dissertations. What doctoral candidate would not want to write something equivalent to these examples?

- History of the English-Speaking Peoples. Winston Churchill. Started in 1937 and finished by 1958, it covered Caesar's invasions of Britain (55 BC) to the start of the First World War (1914).
- The Story of Civilization. Will and Ariel Durant. Covering Western history, the 10,000 pages start with the establishment of civilization and end with the age of Napoleon.

Churchill finished his effort, which started in 1937 and ended in 1958. Not so the Durants. Their masterpiece is incomplete, as they intended to reach the twentieth century. A period of forty-three years, from 1932 to 1975, was not enough time to do it.

DILEMMA OF THE DISSERTATION TOPIC

In the dictionary, "viable" refers to that which is capable of working successfully; that which is feasible, practical, or achievable. In general usage, the word does not impose a time limit. It should for dissertation topics. A dissertation that takes forever is not viable. This situation produces a dilemma:

> Should I choose to solve a problem that is a major contribution to scholarly knowledge or select a narrower topic that is significant but not as noteworthy?

Accompanying the dilemma is a corollary:

> The greater the level of significance of the topic, the smaller the chance of successful completion.

In terms of viability of a dissertation topic, we find a contradiction:

> Why do some of the most intelligent people in terms of IQ scores, when given the right to select any topic in their area of interest and expertise, choose the most cumbersome and complicated topics for their first major research effort?

VIABILITY OF A TOPIC

An idea can generate from one's own professional experience, burning questions in an area of interest, the literature describing issues and unresolved problems, sessions at professional meetings, and discussions with other parties. Wherever it arises, compare it to a short litmus test:

- Feasible. Do you have financial and other resources, access to the data, and the skills needed to complete the analysis and writing?
- Interesting. Do you want more information, to solve a problem, or otherwise spend considerable time investigating it?
- Novel. Would the results be new to the field of knowledge?
- Relevant. Is the issue significant to other scholars or researchers?

VIABILITY

A social sciences doctoral candidate was considering a topic for her dissertation: "Dimensioning the Size of the Ego of Chief Executive Officers of Profit-Making Corporations." Let's run it through a test of viability and see what we uncover.

Question:
What's the biggest challenge to measuring the size of a CEO's ego?
Answer:
Could we ever agree on a working definition of ego, a Freudian construct in a conscious and subconscious structural model of the psyche?

Question:
If we can agree on the meaning of ego, do you want to spend a thousand hours doing this research?
Answer:
Bad question. The first question is "Is this a viable topic for a dissertation? Can you can finish it in six hundred hours? Ten hours a week for forty weeks?

Question:
Ten hours a week for forty weeks is only four hundred hours. What is the link between six hundred hours and ten hours a week for forty weeks?
Answer:
Any successful former doctoral candidate can answer this. The dissertation will require 50 percent more time than expected.

Question:
An experienced director of dissertations estimated that the median length of a humanities, business, or education dissertation is two hundred pages and requires 2,500 hours of work. What does this information tell us?
Answer:
The median doctoral candidate has chosen the wrong topic. Think about it. Such a commitment would tie you up every Saturday and Sunday from 9 a.m. to 6 p.m. for fifteen years. This assumes you get thirty minutes for lunch and two fifteen-minute restroom breaks. If you start on the project in your late twenties, you would be middle aged before you finish.

CRITICAL DECISION POINT: TOPIC

Choose a viable topic. This means:

- Resolve the Dilemma. Choose a narrow but significant topic.
- Recognize the Corollary. Completion trumps significance.
- Avoid the Contradiction. Don't choose the cumbersome and complex over the reality of completion.

EVOLUTION OF A VIABLE TOPIC

A candidate and his director are engaged in a conversation on a dissertation topic.

> Candidate. I am looking forward to working with you. I want to compare the major theories of leadership and determine the similarities and differences in more and less assertive management styles.
>
> Director. It sounds pretty broad. What are you comparing?
>
> Candidate. Servant leadership focusing primarily on helping employees learn, grow, and succeed. The leader shares power and helps people develop and perform as highly as possible.
>
> Director. Is it a standalone theory?
>
> Candidate. Yes. For my study, I want to compare ten theories of leadership. Autocratic, bureaucratic, charismatic, and so forth.
>
> Director. I think your proposal is too broad. Would you consider revising it?
>
> Candidate. Of course.
>
> Director. You are proposing a descriptive dissertation. What is the primary research?
>
> Candidate. I could get data from organizations with and without servant leadership and compare employee turnover and retention as measurements of satisfaction.
>
> Director. Do you realize the difficulty of isolating servant leadership as the independent variable?
>
> Candidate. I could survey people and limit my findings to perceptions.
>
> Director. That would work. What would you ask them?
>
> Candidate. Is servant leadership superior to other theories?
>
> Director. Do you think it would be tricky to validate their answers? What if they are not familiar with servant leadership or other theories?

Candidate. I could ask them to identify the major factors causing an increased interest and awareness in service leadership.

Director. Don't we know that already?

Candidate. I want to refute the criticisms that servant leadership is not unique.

Director. Who cares about that?

Candidate. In my last job, the company followed one theory, then dropped it for servant leadership. I want to know why.

Director. What does that have to do with your dissertation?

Candidate. I want to correct a lack of understanding of servant leadership.

Director. You can do this in your literature review.

Candidate. What do you suggest?

Director. Separate the "crusading" from the primary research. Move on. Develop four to six hypotheses or null hypotheses.

Candidate. How about a narrowing to employee perceptions? A visible concern for the needs and welfare of employees:

- H1. Leads to a high loyalty by customers.
- H2. Engenders trust, thus increasing employee identification with the organization.
- H3. Tends to create an excellent corporate culture.
- H4. Improves employees' performance.
- H5. Improves return on investment.

Director. Okay. Getting closer. Perhaps a Likert scale. Strongly agree, agree, and so forth. Anything else?

Candidate. I might mention one unresolved and significant issue for servant leadership. If it improves employee satisfaction, why is it not more widely used? Could it be that managers do not think it improves performance?

Director. Why would they think that?

Candidate. In my literature review, I discovered a few reasons. Lack of knowledge. Some executives think it equals no or weak leadership. Executives see a religious aspect that scares them. Others are practicing it and don't even know it.

Director. Sounds like fertile ground for significant research.

Three weeks later, the candidate forwards a dissertation proposal. Highlights include:

Title. Servant Leadership and Linkages to Organizational Performance: Customer Satisfaction, Employee Satisfaction, and Return on Investment

Purpose. Determine the level of penetration of servant leadership into profit-making organizations and assess attitudes linking it with organizational performance.

Secondary Research. Review of the literature in categories of participatory democratic, servant, transformational, servant and transformational, and other leadership

Methodology. Written survey of sixty to one hundred targeted employees followed up by confirming interviews with four to six senior executives in profit-making entities.

Significance. Contribute to an understanding of whether practitioners believe that s ervant leadership leads to improved customer satisfaction, employee satisfaction, and return on investment

Question:
  Is the proposal built upon a viable topic?
Answer:
  Tested against our standards, does it:

- resolve the dilemma? Yes. The topic is narrow and significant.
- recognize the corollary? Yes. The narrow topic makes it a job that is not too big to complete.
- avoid the contradiction? Yes. The design is not too cumbersome or complex.

TOPIC ANALYSIS

From this framework, we can perform a formal analysis to narrow down a topic.

- Problem. Does servant leadership improve the performance of low-ranking employees?

- Theory Base. What scholarly work has been done on servant leadership styles?
- Prior Research. Has servant leadership been debunked, supported, or ignored in prior scholarly studies?
- Methodology. How can we gather valid and reliable data on what's perceived to be happening?
- Outcomes. If we use the methodology, what will be the likely findings?
- Importance of the Outcome. Are the findings significant to other researchers or practitioners?

DO YOU NEED A FORMAL PROPOSAL?

After you complete a viable topic analysis, that may not be enough. The institution may want to review your proposal. If the school has no guidelines, consider simply formalizing the topic analysis. Essentially, it contains all the components of a formal proposal.

CONCLUSION

The importance of choosing a viable topic can hardly be exaggerated in the context of completing a dissertation. The topic works when the candidate narrows a significant topic, finds a workable path to conduct the research, and creates a project that is manageable.

Chapter Seventeen

How Can an Advisor Help Create a Workable Proposal? Do We Have Any Tips or Tricks to Share with the Candidates?

If we knew what it was we were doing, it would not be called research, would it?
—Albert Einstein, theoretical physicist

PURPOSE OF A DISSERTATION PROPOSAL

Some professors and most doctoral candidates believe that the purpose of a proposal is to design a dissertation. Nonsense. It is far more important than that. The proposal can help avoid making the wrong kind of error. Two kinds are possible:

- Shirt-Button Error. Occurs when the wrong first step cannot be corrected without returning to the starting point. If the top button does not match the top buttonhole, we cannot correct the mistake when we are halfway down the shirt without undoing all our previous actions.
- Aircraft-in-Flight Error. Happens when we stray off course after we start. If the aircraft deviates from its planned flight pattern, the pilot simply corrects the direction of flight. A long-distance flight involves many small corrections to keep the aircraft headed toward the destination airport.

At every step of designing and proposing a research project, beware of the possibility of making a shirt-button error.

Question:
A candidate proposed a dissertation on corruption in Sicily historically and in modern day. Is this a viable topic?
Answer:
No. The scope is too broad. The possibility of a shirt-button error looms large.

Question:
A candidate has a proposal to survey members of a religious order. The head of the order approved distributing the survey to members. When the candidate asked for the email list, he learned the board of the order withdrew the approval. What happens now?
Answer:
The proposal is invalid. The candidate may find another target survey group and obtain approval to survey its members. If this is successful, the candidate made an aircraft-in-flight error. If it fails, dooming the project, it's a shirt-button error.

SELECTING A TOPIC

The possibility of a shirt-button error starts with selecting a topic. Some guidelines include:

- General Topic. What is the broad area and how does it break down into categories?
- Issues. What are the problems faced, resolved, and outstanding?
- Goal of the Research. What do you want to do?
- Research Questions. What will the study answer?
- Methodology. How will the study gather data?
- Significance. Why should the study be undertaken?

CASE STUDY: COERCIVE LEADERSHIP (CL)

A candidate has identified coercive leadership as a topic of interest for a dissertation. Let's examine how to move from topic to proposal.

Question:
How do you break down the general topic into categories?
Answer:
One way is to use the five Ws augmented by an "H":

- Who? American managers.
- What? Leadership behavior.
- Where? Health care field.
- When? 2012–2017.
- Why? Determine their perceptions of coercive leadership.
- How? Written survey enriched by expert comments.

Question:
What's the key to a successful literature review?
Answer:
The identification of prior research can be divided into four to six major areas of focus. The candidate proposed these categories:

- Coercive Leadership.
- Servant Leadership.
- Autocratic Leadership.
- Bureaucratic Leadership.

GOAL OF THE RESEARCH

The proposal should identify a promising area for research and expresses the project in terms of a goal to be accomplished.

Question:
The candidate selected as a title "An Exploratory Analysis of the Perception of Managers on Coercive Leadership." The goal is "to prove coercive leadership is a more effective style for improving employee performance." Are the title and goal workable?
Answer:
Maybe. The wording of the goal is problematic.

- "Prove?" Does this imply a bias that the researcher believes in an outcome and might shape findings to support it?
- "Coercive leadership is more effective?" Should be "perceived as more effective."
- "More effective?" A comparative survey is far more complex than one that simply seeks to assess effectiveness by itself.
- "Improving employee performance." This may work with a limitation on the absence of a definition of "performance."

HYPOTHESES

A candidate proposed the following research hypotheses for the project:

- CL encourages employees to deal effectively in crisis situations.
- CL prepares managers to deal with problem employees.
- CL encourages organizations to retain only efficient employees.
- CL improves on-the-job performance in a struggling organization.
- CL improves return on investment in a struggling organization.
- CL works effectively in small organizations.
- CL works effectively in large organizations.

Question:
   Do these questions work?
Answer:
   They seem to. They are narrow in focus and scope and deal with crisis and noncrisis situations.

METHODOLOGY

A questionnaire would be used to assess perceptions of coercive behavior comparing males and females, ages of respondents, and amount of work experience. The questionnaire identifies the following categories:

When were you born?	{_} 1960–1980 {_} 1981–2000
What is your gender?	{_} Male {_} Female
Years of work experience since college:	{_} 0 to 4 {_} 5 or more

Question:
   Does this work?
Answer:
   The categories enrich the data and appear to be acceptable.

Question:
   The questionnaire would ask respondents to answer written questions using a Likert scale (strongly agree to strongly disagree). The questions are introduced with the following brief description. Does this work?

> Coercive leadership (CL) achieves goals by bullying and even demeaning followers. Coercive leaders demand immediate compliance with their orders. "Do what I tell you, or else."

Answer:
Yes. A Likert scale gives a measure of qualitative responses and the explanation provides information so respondents do not need to understand coercive leadership prior to receiving the survey form.

DEVELOPING STATEMENTS

The methodology would ask questions to a sample of respondents. The candidate developed questions. The following were challenged by the dissertation director.

> Question. Has your organization allowed, supported, or refuted coercive management behavior?
>
> Comment. Why ask this? The current or prior experience in a CL environment is not a research variable.
>
> Question. Is your current boss a coercive leader?
>
> Comment. Once again, not a research variable.
>
> Question. List two positive and two negative aspects to coercive leadership
>
> Comment: If unfamiliar with CL, no validity.

MISCELLANEOUS ISSUES

As the proposal was being developed, other issues arose.

Question:
The candidate proposed including both profit-making and nonprofit organizations in the survey while pointing out in the research design that the effort "focused" on for-profits. Does this work?
Answer:
No, it's sloppy. You don't "focus" on for-profits. You either do them or you don't.

Question:
The candidate considered whether to exclude nonprofits. Should that be done?

Answer:
The candidate rejected this idea. Some nonprofits are enormous, as is the case for the Red Cross and universities. They have characteristics of for-profit businesses. Also, respondents would be forced to self-identify. If a potential respondent worked three years for the Peace Corps and three months for IBM, would the individual identify as nonprofit or for-profit? Findings in such a situation cannot be valid in a framework of limiting them to for-profits.

Question:
Should the questionnaire ask for industry designation so research could be sliced to show differences in health care, manufacturing, and other lines of business?
Answer:
No. The research cannot be validated from a self-identified industry classification. Consider a respondent who works at a bottled water company. What is the industry?

Question:
Should the questionnaire ask for the number of employees or whether the company is national or international?
Answer:
No. Also validity problems. If a respondent works in the accounting unit in New York for Home Depot, how many employees are in the unit? Is it national or international?

CIRCLING BACK

With the questionnaire designed, the candidate took a look back at the introductory material.

Question:
The purpose is to improve an understanding of the perception of CL by managers and professionals in categories of men, women, younger, and older respondents. Does this match the data gathering?
Answer:
It seems to.

Question:
The contribution is to add to the evidence of whether these groups actually perceive a link between CL practices and improved performance. Does this match the data gathering?

Answer:
It seems to.

Question:
The significance is that a better understanding of the existence or absence of such a link will be valuable for future scholarly research as well as improving business practices. Does this match the data gathering?
Answer:
It seems to.

Question:
During methodology discussions, a question arose about the contribution of the research. Should the study also examine a link between acceptance of the CL philosophy and its adoption in organizations?
Answer:
The idea was rejected. This is a separate dissertation.

Question:
Should the hypotheses be combined into one such as "CL improves performance by focusing employees on crises when survival is at stake?"
Answer:
No. It is a stronger design to test four to six hypotheses on narrow links between independent and dependent variables. After tabulating the results, you can interpret them suggesting extension into a larger picture.

Question:
As formulated, the dissertation now answers "What are perceptions of coercive behavior in problem or crisis situations and small or large organizations?" Should it also answer the following?

- Why is CL practiced in noncrisis situations?
- How widely understood is CL?
- What specific issues limit its acceptance when appropriate for survival?

Answer:
No. Parenthetically, these three research questions could be three separate dissertations using a grounded theory approach.

Chapter 17

CONCLUSION

The process of building a dissertation proposal contains key elements that are identified, evaluated, and revised until a valid and reliable research methodology is developed on a viable dissertation topic.

Chapter Eighteen

We Know Corruption Is Bad but Is It a Suitable Topic for a Doctoral Dissertation? How Should We Decide?

> The American Republic will endure until the day Congress discovers that it can bribe the public with the public's money.
> —Alexis de Tocqueville, French historian

We do not have to define "corruption" to discuss it. U.S. Supreme Court Justice Potter Stewart paved the way in 1964 when he said, "I don't know how to define it, but I know it when I see it." He was talking about obscenity but might as well have been talking about corruption. We only have to start telling a story and we can feel that something is not right.

Such an attitude may work for a U.S. Supreme Court Justice. It fails for a doctoral candidate who must write a dissertation. Let's look at it from a scholarly research perspective.

DEFINITION OF BUSINESS

A doctoral candidate wants to write a definitive dissertation about "corrupt business." The following discussion takes place:

Mentor. How can I help you?

Candidate. I think businesses are corrupt. I want to write the definitive research study that proves the case.

Mentor. What's a business?

Candidate. Providing services in exchange for money.

Mentor. Is this activity corrupt?

Candidate. Not the activity. The people who engage in it.

Mentor. Buyers and sellers?

Candidate. No. Just sellers.

Mentor. Owners, officers, and employees of organizations?

Candidate. Yes.

Mentor. What if a business does not have owners?

Candidate. All businesses have owners.

Mentor. Who owns the American Red Cross, U.S. Methodist Church, Seattle University, and Little League baseball?

Candidate. They are not businesses.

Mentor. But they provide services.

Candidate. You're confusing me.

Question:
So what's the problem?
Answer:
The scope of the research effort is too broad.

DEFINITION OF CORRUPTION

The role of the mentor continues.

Mentor. What do you mean by corruption?

Candidate. I think everyone knows that corruption refers to dishonest or fraudulent conduct by those in power. It typically involves bribery.

Mentor. Like bribing a politician? Like awarding a contract to build municipal water treatment plant?

Candidate. Exactly.

Mentor. How is this action corrupt?

Candidate. The politician approves giving the contract to a friend and takes a bribe for doing it.

Mentor. Got it. How does it work for a business?

Candidate. The business pays the bribe.

Mentor. What if all bidders bribe the politician? Is that the system or is it corruption?

Candidate. It is corruption.

Mentor. Dishonest means untrustworthy, unfair, unjust, or unethical. If all bidders know the arrangement, how is it dishonest?

Candidate. It harms citizens whose taxes are wasted on bribes.

Mentor. So who is corrupt? The politician who demands a bribe or the business when everyone knows a bribe is required to obtain the contract?

Candidate. The whole system is corrupt.

Mentor. So what's the point of the research on business corruption?

Question:
How should the candidate answer the question?
Answer:
The candidate needs to acknowledge the problem. Corruption in business can be a fertile area for research but the topic needs to be structured.

SOURCES OF CORRUPTION

We can start with sources of bad behavior:

- Outlaw Trade. Business practices and activities that are harmful or illegal to a country, economy, and citizens.
- Politics. Harmful actions of governments, public agencies, the police, and the courts.
- Unethical Behavior. Activities that violate moral principles and acceptable behavior.
- Economic Corruption. Practices or behaviors that deprive individuals of their property or livelihood.

CATEGORIES OF CORRUPTION

A slightly different approach leads to corruption by category.

- Political Corruption. When government officials seek illegitimate personal gain from their official positions.
- Organizational Corruption. When profit or nonprofit units abuse suppliers, customers, employees, and even unrelated parties.
- Legal Corruption. Acts by a public official or private person inconsistent with official duty or the rights of others under the law.
- Nepotism and Cronyism. Acts of favoritism granted to relatives or friends without regard for their merit.
- Involuntary Gifts as Corruption. Improper monetary or other gifts to officials or business decision makers.

Question:
   A Chinese entrepreneur started a food products exporting firm. His nephew was sent to school in Toronto. Upon graduation and with no work experience, the nephew was named the chief executive officer of Canadian operations. Is this corruption?
Answer:
   Not in the Chinese cultural context where trust, loyalty, and hard work are paramount. Family members have long-term obligations to one another that make nepotism perfectly legitimate.

Question:
   An official in Africa is soliciting bids for a government contract. He awards the contract to an old friend rather than to the low bidder. Is this an example of cronyism?
Answer:
   Sure. Because of the personal relationship, he may be confident that the friend will do the job right. He also knows the friend is reasonable if the parties need to discuss problems or changes in the agreement. Responsible cronyism, like responsible nepotism, may not be corruption at all.

Question:
   In the United States, cities such as Chicago and Baltimore have a long history of "walk-around money." Politicians gave money to citizens to vote for them. When elected, the officials use government funds to take care of the neediest. Is this an example of corruption?
Answer:
   Maybe not. Though corruption accompanies the practice in many cases, beneficial results accrue to citizens of both cities.

THE RESEARCH PROBLEM

With the preceding foundation, the researcher is encouraged to approach corruption in a formal framework without abrupt assumptions. We have definitions, sources, and categories. We do not have a focus. That's our next step.

BUSINESS CORRUPTION

Corruption in the global business environment is not a simple statement that something is wrong. Let's focus it. To be defined as corruption, we must have:

- A Goal. An organized system must have a goal, specifically trying to achieve recognizable objectives that improve an organization, social group, or community.
- Misbehavior. One or more individuals or entities of the system must engage in a behavior that affects the system.
- System Damage. The behavior must undermine the goal of the system. It must have a negative impact, either immediately or long term.
- Stakeholder Harm. The misbehavior must hurt stakeholders. That is, it must harm both individuals who depend on the system and diminish the viability of the system itself.

If any one of these elements is missing, we may have bad behavior and negative consequences, but we will not consider it to be corruption. Done with that.

NARROW DOWN THE TOPIC

Corruption is a broad concept. One interesting area deals with bribery. Many people have commented on it.

> Never underestimate the effectiveness of a straight cash bribe.
> —Claude Cockburn, twentieth-century British journalist and writer

> A fine is a bribe paid by a rich man to escape the lawful penalty of his crime.
> —H. L. Mencken, American journalist and critic

> Until the nineteen-seventies, Western countries paid little attention to . . . bribery. In some European countries, businesses were even allowed to deduct bribes as an expense.
> —James Surowiecki, journalist

DEFINITION OF BRIBERY

Mr. Cockburn, Mr. Mencken, and Mr. Surowiecki are speaking about bribes without a definition. Which definition does each intend from the two choices given us by the Merriam-Webster online dictionary?

- Definition #1. Something that serves to induce or influence.
- Definition #2. Money or favor given or promised to influence the judgment or conduct of a person in a position of trust.

A small sum of money given to a waiter or baggage handler as a reward for good service is quite different from the payment to a government official to break a law. To capture the difference, we define bribery under the following conditions:

- Purpose. Someone seeks to influence the judgment or conduct of another person.
- Monetary Value. The bribe has a cash value.
- Corrupt Act. The action contains an element of corruption.

No problem with purpose or monetary value. Everyone knows what they mean. But a "corrupt act?" What's that?

Fortunately, our researcher already defined it. It must occur in a system with a goal and be a misbehavior because it causes damage to the system and harm to its stakeholders. Absent these characteristics, a payment for influence or favor is simply a tip, a reward, or a gift.

This approach does not preclude the possibility that a reward or gift may be illegal. Payments to government officials that are illegal in some jurisdictions are customary and usual behavior in others. A conflict arises when a company makes a payment that is legal at home but is a felony when given in another country.

NARROWING THE DISCUSSION

If we now understand corruption, where do we go? Let's continue the discussion.

Mentor. What's the purpose of your research?

Candidate. Being from Kenya, I want to advance an understanding of economic development in Africa.

Mentor. What's the area of your proposed dissertation?

Candidate. A business corruption case study.

Mentor. What area of the Kenyan economy interests you?

Candidate. The cell phone market.

Mentor. What time period?

Candidate. From 2006 to 2012.

Mentor. What happened in that period?

Candidate. Three companies evolved to develop the market.

Mentor. How about a dissertation on corruption in the development of the cell phone market in Kenya during the period from 2006 to 2012?

LITERATURE REVIEW CATEGORIES

With the narrow perspective on corruption in the cell phone market in Kenya, we can identify categories for the literature review. How about choosing from among the following?

- Outlaw Trade. Illegal practices and activities that do not originate with the public sector.
- Politics. Harmful actions of governments, public agencies, the police, and the courts.
- Unethical Behavior. Violations of cultural and moral expectations.
- Economic Corruption. Practices or behaviors that deprive individuals or organizations of their property or livelihood.
- Political Corruption. Government officials seek illegitimate gain from their positions.
- Organizational Corruption. Nongovernmental units abuse others.
- Legal Corruption. Individuals gain advantage inconsistent with official duty or the rights of others.
- Nepotism and Cronyism. Favoritism to relatives or friends without regard to merit.

CONCLUSION

We can define corruption. We can narrow the scope to bribery and define the term. We can continue the process of research carefully delineating concepts, building upon foundations in carefully structured frameworks, and leading our research efforts to find results that form a scholarly work of research. This is the start of academic scholarship.

Chapter Nineteen

Have You Heard Any Good Dissertation Stories Lately? Would You Like One to Finish This Journey?

Love all, trust a few, do wrong to none.
—William Shakespeare, British author

INSPIRATION FROM SHAKESPEARE

Perhaps you are familiar with the above quote from Shakespeare. In the play, Helena, the low-born ward of a French countess, is in love with the countess's son Bertram, who is indifferent to her. After she wins favor of the king, Bertram is forced to marry her. It is not working well and, after trials and tribulations, then it does. Bertram, impressed by her efforts, swears his love to her. Thus all ends well.

We have a parallel situation when, after a lengthy journey, the oral defense is over. You are outside the room waiting for the verdict. The chair of the dissertation committee invites you back into the room and says, "Congratulations doctor," followed by your last name. At this point, everything seems worthwhile. Or in the language of the Bard, "All's well that ends well."

To achieve that outcome with a reduced level of stress and effort, let's share a personal journey: my own dissertation story under the guidance of a wise and helpful director.

Chapter 19

A DISSERTATION JOURNEY

Year one. The start of doctoral coursework in September at George Washington University was preceded by a meeting with Paul. Newly minted himself as a doctor, he was an expert on international finance. A discussion took place:

> Candidate. I am interested in doing my dissertation on political risk affecting project financing using Eurobonds.
>
> Paul. I will work with you only if you can define "political."

Three months later. Another discussion.

> Candidate. "Political" is something relating to the government or the public affairs of a country or maybe the ideas or strategies of a particular party or people in politics.
>
> Paul. Can you use that in a hypothesis?
>
> Candidate. Sure. Hypothesis: Political risk causes companies to pay more for their long-term financing.
>
> Paul. Can you isolate political risk?
>
> Candidate. Yes. First, measure the level of turmoil in a few countries' politics. Then link it to interest rates affecting their currencies during a fixed period. Compare the situation to interest rates in a less turbulent period for the countries. Conclude on the impact of political turmoil on interest rates.
>
> Paul. Would you have to adjust your data for exchange rate fluctuations with the different currencies?
>
> Candidate. Of course.
>
> Paul. So first you find comparable situations in a couple of countries, measure precisely the level of political turmoil, gather interest rates and exchange rates from financial markets, and use a statistical algorithm to process levels and changes in political risk, interest rates, and exchange rate changes, and draw significant conclusions on correlation or causation on political risk and the cost of financing?
>
> Candidate. It sounds like a lot.

Paul. It does not sound like a viable project to me.

Candidate. What do you suggest?

Paul. Write a paper for one of your courses on the Eurobond market. Write one for another course on exchange rates and long-term financing. Write down in APA format all your references and link them to specific quotes and viewpoints in the two papers.

Candidate. What then?

Paul. Come back and talk to me.

Year two. More course work. Another discussion.

Candidate. I did what you said. Here are the two papers. Do you want to read them?

Paul. No. Now write two more papers for your courses. One should be a descriptive paper on the features and mechanisms of the Eurobond market. The other should be an analytical paper on interest rates and exchange rate fluctuations in international finance.

Candidate. Then come back and talk to you?

Paul. Yep.

Six more months.

Candidate. I did what you said.

Paul. Now what?

Candidate. I am researching a multicountry investment borrowing in one currency and converting it for investment in a project in another country. I built and tested a model comparing exchange rate fluctuations, inflation, and interest rates to develop an optimal combination of the currency to borrow and invest for maximum discounted cash flow internal rate of return.

Paul. What do you have?

Candidate. A linear regression equation $DRes = f(Pr^8{}_9, Y_r)$ that I tested using a standard regression program adjusted for degrees of freedom. Five countries were included in the scope of the testing: United States,

United Kingdom, Germany, France, and Japan. The time period was from 1958 to 1969. My calculations show three types of correlation using a linear regression calculation. One covers year-to-year correlations with no lag. I got the following results for the first correlation.

Paul. Okay.

Findings: Year-to-Year Correlations with No Lag

Germany

$\Delta \text{Res} = -.14 - 3.23\text{Pr} / 1.2 + 1.70\text{Yr} / .48 \ R^2 = 67\%$

United States

$\Delta \text{Res} = -.038 + .281\text{Pr} / 1.0 + .663\text{Yr} / 1.2 \ R^2 = 10\%$

United Kingdom

$\Delta \text{Res} = -.141 - 5.66\text{Pr} / 7.8 - 2.54\text{Yr} / 2.9 \ R^2 = 12\%$

France

$\Delta \text{Res} = -.031 + 1.66\text{Pr} / 8.9 + 1.85\text{Yr} / 9.1 \ R^2 = 2\%$

Japan

$\Delta \text{Res} = .983 - 13.8\text{Pr} / 14 - 5.30\text{Yr} / 4.4 \ R^2 = 18\%$

Candidate. Am I on the right track? Will this model be accepted by a doctoral committee at the oral defense?

Director. I have no idea. At least, you're not fooling around trying to do something with global politics. Finish the dissertation and let me see it.

Year three. Paul leaves the faculty and takes a position at the International Monetary Fund. His work was largely done. A dissertation titled "Eurobond Financing and Currency Appraisal Aspects of International Financing" was submitted and defended. The journey was over. Paul sat as the outside reader at the oral defense. "All's well . . ."

LESSONS LEARNED

If you choose the right advisor, you will work with someone who helps without taking over, provides guidance as needed, and allows you to move forward.

CONCLUSION

All roads lead you to where you are going. Some just take a little longer. It helps to have a roadmap, compass, and even GPS capability. Not to mention someone like Paul who can smooth the bumps of the journey.

Chapter Twenty

How Should You Structure a Dissertation? Is It Important to Know Where You Are Going?

> My mission in life is not merely to survive, but to thrive; and to do so with some passion, some compassion, some humor, and some style.
> —Maya Angelou, American poet

DISSERTATION PROPOSAL

You start with a proposal, even if not formally required to complete one. It answers questions in three areas:

- Research Problem. Is it important, original, and supported by sound hypotheses?
- Literature Review. Is it solid and pertinent as a foundation for the research?
- Research Methodology. Is it consistent with the objectives? Does it specify all of the steps? Will it produce valid and reliable data?

An example is twelve to fifteen pages organized in sections:

- Intended Research. Identify an issue.
- Annotated Past Scholarship. Outline prior academic research.
- Research Design. Describe an approach to collect and analyze data.
- Conduct of the Research. Fulfill a formal research design.
- Findings. Interpret the data and present findings.

DISSERTATION STRUCTURE

After you have your mind around the proposal, outline the dissertation.

Introductory Material

- Title and Declaration Pages.
- Abstract. Single spaced, 300 to 400 words, describing the issue, objectives of the study, methods used, significance of the study, findings, limitations, and areas for further research.
- Dedications and Acknowledgments. Optional.
- Table of Contents. Chapter headings and page numbers.

Chapters

1. Introduction and Theoretical Framework

   - Statement of the Problem. The context and theoretical framework in clear language.
   - Purpose of the Study.
   - Significance of the Study.
   - Limitations of the Study.
   - Summary.

2. Review of the Literature

   - Introduction.
   - Categories. Research findings in four to six groupings by topical area.
   - Summary. A paragraph or two to recap the chapter.

3. Research Methods

   - Introduction. A sentence describing major headings in order.
   - Methodology. Qualitative, quantitative, or mixed method. Questions or hypotheses.
   - Design. Methods and procedures. What did the researcher do? What were the conditions?
   - Collection of Data.
   - Sampling. Random, convenience, or purposive structure. Define the population. Reliability and validity of results.
   - IRB Compliance. If needed, explanation of meeting high ethical standards and no harm to human subjects.

- Instrumentation. A description of validity and reliability of instruments used for data collection.
- Data Timetable. Activities collecting data.
- Summary. Recap the chapter.

4. Findings

    - Introductory Statement. Explains how findings will be presented.
    - Findings for Each Question or Hypothesis. Presentation and interpretation of data separately for each research item. Tables and figures added as appropriate.
    - Significance. Interpretation of the significance or lack of significance for each item. Include support or refutation of findings to the existing literature. Include limitations on validity and reliability.
    - Future Research. Describe new insights and implications for theory and practice. Suggest research needed to augment, refine, or plug gaps in findings.
    - Summary. A paragraph or two to recap the chapter.

5. Appendices

    - List of Tables. (Separate page.) In the order in which they occur numbered by chapter.
    - List of Figures. (Separate page.) In the order in which they occur numbered by chapter.
    - List of Abbreviations. (Separate page.) In alphabetical order.
    - Miscellaneous. Possibilities are questionnaires, measuring instruments, interview schedules, large tables of data, notes on methods used, or list of copyrighted items or material.

CONSIDER THE EXPECTATIONS OF THE DIRECTOR

The dissertation director or doctoral committee will be looking for certain things:

1. Compliance with Proposal

    - Research problem.
    - Literature review.
    - Methodology.

2. Analysis of the Results

- Validity of the findings.
- Reliability of the findings
- Significance of the finding.
- Value of the findings.

3. Presentation of the Research and Results

    - Conformity with institutional guidelines on format.
    - Accuracy and precision of data, interpretation, and findings.
    - Clear writing style.

Index

abductive approach to scholarship, 18
absence of prior research, limitation, 124
abuses, Joshua Woods' application, 9
academic: knowledge, 20; scholarship, 18
access, dissertation obstacle, 125
administrator agreement with "higher" standards, 40
advisor: discussions, examples, 97; dissertation, 91; incorporating the, 97
aircraft-in-flight error, 145
all but dissertation (ABD), 29
alternative hypothesis, defined, 103
apprentice, 27
apprenticeship period of scholarship, 30
approvals dissertation, 131
approximation, 18
areas of BASSE research, 21
areas of scholarship, 20
attribute of variables, defined, 74, 75
autodidact route to academic scholarship, 24
available time, dissertation obstacle, 125

background to the scholarly crisis, 37
baseball data organized into information, 84
basketball, interpreting data, 86
Beall's list, predatory journals, 43
bias, underlying factors,, 87
book reviews and other writings, 32

business, arts, social sciences, and education (BASSE), 21

case control, defined, 104
case study—coercive leadership (cl), 146
categories of academic scholarship, 23
causal: relationship, 76; research, 22; scholarship, 20
causation, 111
citation: format sheet, 94; in dissertation, 93, 94
coefficient of determination, defined, 112
coefficient of multiple correlation, defined, 112
cognitive intelligence, 64
cognitively smarter, American teenager?, 65
cohort study, defined, 104
common questions on writing dissertations, 90
completion of the dissertation, 132, 135
complexity of the statistics, beware, 114
comprehensive background study, dissertation, 73
concurrent validity, 75
conference proceedings, 31
confidence interval, defined, 120
confidence level, defined, 120
conscious bias, 87
construct, validity, 82
contagiousness, tipping point, 53

content, validity, 53
contingent faculty., 11
continuing faculty, 11
control group, defined, 104
convenience sample, defined, 118
correlated relationship, 76
correlation, 111; coefficient, defined, 112; measures, 112
correlational research, 22
crisis, abuses started, 9
crisis, aspects of, x
cross-sectional study, defined, 101
curious about obscure facts?, 69

data: availability limitation, 124; corruption, 82; defined, 81; discrimination, 83; integrity, 82; loss, 82; sources, 82, 83; tell the story with, 85
data. incomplete, deceptive, intensity of, 86
data story, Shane Battier, basketball, 85
deceptive data, 86
deduction fallacy, 106
deductive: approach to scholarship, 18; research, 17, 117
dependent variable, defined, 74
descriptive: scholarship, 20, 22; statistics, 110; study, 105
dilemma of the dissertation topic, 138
directional hypothesis, defined, 103
discipline area knowledge, 20
disruption in the academy, 10
disruptive view, academic scholarship, 15
dissertation: journey, 162; phase scholarship, 33; purpose of, 49; quick start, 34; reforms, 72; structure, 168; writing, getting a grip, 130
dissertation director, beware of wrong, 132
dissertation proposal, 167; do you need a?, 143
dissertation story, Mafia, (disguised), 133
doctoral degree holders, 58

early Christian theologians, 38
edge for emotional intelligence, 65
elite colleges, 3
emotional: bias, 87; intelligence, 64
empirical research, 21

exactitude, 18
exhaustive attributes, variables, 75
expectations of the director, 169
experimental: research, 22; study, 106
external, validity, 106

faculty crisis, 11
findings, importance of and exaggerations, 126
flawed findings in dissertations, 126
Fordham University, 5
foreseeing obstacles with dissertations, 125
formal knowledge, 20

general interest publications, 32, 46
general knowledge, 20, 65
great scholarship, not dissertations, 137
grounded theory, 21

Harvard undergraduates, family income of, 4
hazing, doctoral candidate, 51
heterogeneous population, defined, 118
hidden ailment, scholarly research, 37
high school graduates (2016), 3
higher education today, ix
hoax, article, John Bohannon, 43
homogeneous population, defined, 118
hypothesis, defined, 102

idiographic research, 22
in-text citation, 93
incomplete data, 86
independent variable, defined, 74
individual justice, 38
induction fallacy, 106
inductive approach to scholarship, 18
inductive research, 19, 117
inference in research, 77
information, defined, 81
inquiry, 18
insignificant results, dissertation, 126
inspiration from Shakespeare, 161
intensity of data, 86
intern, 27
internal, validity, 78
intuition, research reasoning, 74
inverse relationship, 76
issues with contingent faculty, 12

journeyman, 27

knowledge, defined, 81

lateral thinking, 74
length, dissertation, 90
liberation period of scholarship, 31
linear thinking, 74
literature citation, 93
little things, big difference, 55
longitudinal study, defined, 101

Mafia dissertation story, (disguised), 133
master craftsman, 27
measurement, results, 78
medieval: research structure, 27; universities, 38
mentor overload, dissertation, 72
methodology overload, dissertation, 72, 124
mixed method scholarship, 20
motives to conduct scholarly research, 23
mutually exclusive attributes, variables, 75

negative relationship, 76
negative results, significance of, 124
new research, limitation, 124
nomothetic research, 21
non-directional hypothesis, defined, 103
non-response bias, 87
nonprobability sample, defined, 119
null hypothesis, defined, 103

obscure knowledge, 68
one-tail hypothesis, defined, 103
organize limitations, 126
original research, dissertation, 73

personal bias, dissertation obstacle, 125
Phoenix, University of, 7
popular magazines, 46
population of sample group, 118
positive relationship, 76
post-doctoral scholarship, 33
pre-Christian concepts scholarship, 38
predatory journals, 43
predatory journals, Beall's list, 43
predictive validity, 43
premise of this book, xii

preproposal, dissertation examples, 94
preproposal: a dissertation on leadership, 95
preproposal: a dissertation on management, 96
preproposal: dissertation on economic development, 95
preproposal statement, dissertation, 94
primary source data, 82
probabilistic research, 22
probability is not certainty, 120
probability sample, defined, 119
professional: books, 32; trade journals, 32; working papers, 32
professoriate bar, raising it, 39
professors as the heirs of Plato, 38
prospective study, defined, 104
publications on Sense list (2016), 47
publishing your dissertation findings, 34
purpose: of a dissertation, 49; of a dissertation proposal, 145
purposive sampling, 110
Pyne, Derek, predatory journal articles assessment, 44

qualitative research, 19, 20
quantitative research, 19, 20
quota sample, defined, 118

random sample, 118; defined, 118
realistic view cognitive intelligence, 65
realities of the dissertation, 132
reality of data sources, 83
redundancy in dissertation, 92
reference books, writing dissertations, 89
reflection on dissertation, 135
reforming the doctoral dissertation, 59
relationship management, 71
relationships, 76
reliability, defined, 77
renaissance philosophers, scholarship, 38
repeatability, defined, 78
reproducibility, defined, 78
research affliction, start of, 44
research design—just in case, 56; —just in time, 56
research fallacy, 106
research limitations, 123

research methodology: courses, 55; advice from advisor, 103
research reasoning, 74
resolving statistical validity, case study, 114
retrospective knowledge, limitation, 124
retrospective study, defined, 104
right context, tipping point, 53
right message, tipping point, 53
right people, tipping point, 53
right places to publish?, 47

sample size limitation, 123
samples in research, using, 119
sampling, defined, 117
sampling categories, 118
sampling error, defined, 120
scholar, succeeding as a, 40
scholarly: crisis, background to, 37; journals, 31, 42
scholarly research, x, 18, 19; who reads?, 41
scholarly researchers, 23
scholarship: and intelligence, 71; of application, 23; of discovery, 23; of integration, 23; of learning, 23; view of doctoral, 33; view of Fordham, SNHU, Phoenix,, 6
science, technology, engineering, and mathematics (STEM), 21
second reader dissertation, 91
secondary source data, 82
selecting a dissertation topic, 146
self-awareness, 71
self-management, 71
self-reported data, limitation, 124
Sense publishing, scholarly journals, 42
Sense publishing categories, 47
sequential, research reasoning, 74
shirt-button error, 145
should you write a dissertation?, 73
significance defined, 110
significant in research, definition, 110
significant issue, dissertation, 73
simple sample, 118
social: awareness, 71; desirability bias, 87; justice, 38
Sokal hoax, x

Southern New Hampshire University (SNHU), 6
stages of scholarly research, 29
stakeholder views, contingent faculty, 13
statistical inference, 110
statistical significance, case study:, 110, 112
statistically significant, defined, 119
statistics and purposive sampling, 109
statistics in scholarly research, 122
stratified sample, defined, 118
subconscious influence, 87
systematic sample, defined, 118
Szust hoax application, editorial boards, 43

t-test, defined, 120
tenure and depression, 30
tenured and tenure track faculty views, contingent faculty, 14
theoretical research, 21
thesis versus dissertation, 49
time to completion, doctoral degree, 52
time, research in, 101
timetable for writing dissertation, 89
tipping point in the academy, 53
tips on limitations, 126
today's scholarship, development of, 39
topic, critical decision point, 139
topic, selection for dissertation, 130
topic of dissertation: analysis, 142; evolution of, 140
trade journals, 46
tuition, sample costs:, 57
two-tail hypothesis, defined, 103

Ulrich's list, scholarly journals, 42
Ulrich's peer-reviewed list, 47
underlying factors and bias, 86, 87
unhappy associate professors, 28

validity, defined, 77, 78
variable, defined, 74
variables, attributes of, 75
viability of a dissertation topic, 138
view of doctoral scholarship, 33
view of scholarship, Fordham, SNHU, Phoenix, 6
violence in citation, 94

Wikipedia, places to publish, 47

writing dissertation, getting a grip, 130

About the Author

John J. Hampton is a professor of business at St. Peter's University in New Jersey and a principal in the Princeton Consulting Group. He is the author of some thirty books and multiple journal articles and opinion pieces, many of them dealing with higher education. He was dean of the schools of business at Seton Hall and Connecticut State universities and provost of the College of Insurance and SUNY Maritime College in New York City. He works closely with master's thesis and doctoral dissertation candidates from the International School of Management (ISM) in Paris and is a member of the editorial board of the *Journal of International Business*.

www.ingramcontent.com/pod-product-compliance
Lightning Source LLC
Chambersburg PA
CBHW021850300426
44115CB00005B/94